FAMIL
WALKS

CHILTERNS - NORTH

Nick Moon

This book is one of a series of two which provide a comprehensive coverage of walks throughout the whole of the Chiltern area. The walks included vary in length from 1.8 to 5.5 miles, but are mainly in the 3- to 5-mile range which is ideal for families with children, less experienced walkers or short winter afternoons.

Each walk text gives details of nearby places of interest and is accompanied by a specially drawn map of the route which also indicates local pubs and a skeleton road network.

The author, Nick Moon, has lived in or regularly visited the Chilterns all his life and has, for 25 years, been an active member of the Chiltern Society's Rights of Way Group, which seeks to protect and improve the area's footpath and bridleway network. Thanks to the help and encouragement of the late Don Gresswell MBE, he was introduced to the writing of books of walks and has since written or contributed to a number of publications in this field.

OTHER PUBLICATIONS BY NICK MOON

Family Walks
Family Walks 1 :   Chilterns - South : Book Castle 1997
Family Walks 2 :   Chilterns - North : Book Castle 1998

Chiltern Walks Trilogy
Chiltern Walks 1:   Hertfordshire, Bedfordshire and
                      North Buckinghamshire:
                      Book Castle (new edition) 1996
Chiltern Walks 2 :   Buckinghamshire:
                      Book Castle (new edition) 1997
Chiltern Walks 3 :   Oxfordshire and West Buckinghamshire:
                      Book Castle (new edition) 1996

Oxfordshire Walks
Oxfordshire Walks 1: Oxford, The Cotswolds and The Cherwell
                     Valley: Book Castle (new edition) 1998
Oxfordshire Walks 2: Oxford, The Downs and The Thames Valley:
                     Book Castle 1995

Other Complete Books
Walks for Motorists: Chilterns (Southern Area):
                      Frederick Warne 1979
Walks for Motorists: Chilterns (Northern Area):
                      Frederick Warne 1979
Walks in the Hertfordshire Chilterns: Shire 1986

First published April 1998
by The Book Castle
12 Church Street, Dunstable, Bedfordshire.

© Nick Moon, 1998

Printed in Great Britain by Antony Rowe Ltd., Chippenham, Wilts.

ISBN 1 871 199 68 9

Contents

	Page
Introduction	5
Index Maps	8
Country Code	10

FAMILY WALKS 1 : CHILTERNS - NORTH
LIST OF WALKS

Title		Miles	Km	Page
No. 1 : Croxley Green		5.3	8.6	11
No. 2 : Abbot's Langley		4.5	7.3	15
No. 3 : Apsley		4.8	7.8	20
No. 4 : Ley Hill		4.3	7.0	24
No. 5 : Cholesbury	(A)	4.7	7.6	28
	(B)	2.8	4.5	
No. 6 : Chartridge		4.7	7.5	33
No. 7 : Hyde Heath		4.0	6.5	37
No. 8 : Great Missenden		3.6	5.8	41
No. 9 : Hampden Row	(A)	4.7	7.5	45
	(B)	4.5	7.3	
No. 10 : Great Kimble		4.1	6.6	50
No. 11 : Wendover		5.4	8.8	54
No. 12 : Wendover Woods		5.3	8.6	58
No. 13 : Wilstone		4.7	7.5	62
No. 14 : Ivinghoe	(A)	4.3	6.9	67
	(B)	4.3	6.9	
No. 15 : Tring Station		4.1	6.6	71
No. 16 : Berkhamsted (Bank Mill)		5.1	8.2	75
No. 17 : Berkhamsted Common		3.8	6.2	79
No. 18 : Great Gaddesden		5.0	8.1	83
No. 19 : Piccott's End		4.9	8.0	87
No. 20 : Flamstead		5.5	8.9	91
No. 21 : Caddington		5.4	8.7	95
No. 22 : Dunstable Downs	(A)	3.9	6.4	99
	(B)	1.8	3.0	
	(C)	2.4	3.8	
No. 23 : Totternhoe Knolls	(A)	3.8	6.1	103
	(B)	3.6	5.9	

3

Title		Miles	Km	Page
No. 24 : Houghton Regis		4.8	7.8	107
No. 25 : Sundon Hills		5.3	8.6	112
No. 26 : Barton-le-Clay		2.3	3.7	116
No. 27 : Pirton		4.9	7.9	120
No. 28 : Great Offley	(A)	5.4	8.8	124
	(B)	4.4	7.2	
No. 29 : Stopsley	(A)	5.0	8.1	128
	(B)	3.2	5.2	
No. 30 : Breachwood Green	(A)	5.1	8.2	132
	(B)	4.2	6.8	
	(C)	2.5	4.0	
Index of Place Names				137

POSSIBLE LONGER WALKS PRODUCED BY COMBINING WALKS DESCRIBED IN THE BOOK

Walks	Miles	Km
5A + 11 + 12	16.4	26.4
5A + 12	10.4	16.7
11 + 12	11.4	18.3

Cover photograph : © Nick Moon. View towards Hazeldene Farm, near Chesham. (Walk 6)

Introduction

This book of walks is one of two covering the whole of the Chilterns from the Goring Gap on the River Thames to the Hitchin Gap in North Hertfordshire. The part covered by this volume is that roughly north of a line from Princes Risborough in the west through Amersham to Rickmansworth in the east and so includes the whole of the Bedfordshire Chilterns, all but the southern tip of the Hertfordshire Chilterns and a substantial part of the Buckinghamshire Chilterns.

To the west and north, the area is bounded by the high Chiltern escarpment with its fine views, its variety of open downland, woodland and scrub and its pleasant foothills with views towards the ridge; while, to the east, is a rather arbitrary and subjective line separating the more pronounced hills of the Chilterns from the lower rolling hills of central and eastern Hertfordshire, running from Hitchin in the north by way of Harpenden and St. Albans to Watford in the south.

Within this area are a number of ranges of hills separated by the river valleys traditionally followed by the radial transport arteries out of London, each of which has its own unique character. Southwest of the Wendover Gap and Misbourne Valley is the Chiltern heartland of the Hampden country with the wide Hampden Bottom and considerable areas of traditional Chiltern beechwoods. North of the Misbourne and west of the Chess valley is a remote area of narrow, steep-sided ridges and bottoms, much of which is less wooded than the Hampden country, while to the east of Chesham is the quiet Hertfordshire upland plateau around Chipperfield which has stayed remarkably rural despite its close proximity to London. To the north of the Bulbourne and west of the Gade valleys is the range of hills dominated by the National Trust´s Ashridge Estate with its extensive woodland, downland and open commons, while to the east of the Gade and on both sides of the Ver valley are areas of quiet upland plateau with largely arable land interspersed with small woods. Finally to the east of Luton is the remote area around Lilley Bottom, which, though somewhat less wooded and seemingly less well-known to walkers, in many ways resembles the Hampden country at the other end of the book´s area of coverage.

The basic walks in this book are in the 2 - 5.5 mile range which is ideal for families, less experienced walkers or short winter afternoons and there are a number of shorter versions given which may be preferable for those with younger children or when time is short. In addition, details of several possible combinations of walks of up to 16.4 miles are provided for those wishing to take a longer walk but those requiring more are advised to try the 'Chiltern Walks` series by the same author which contain basic walks in the 5 - 10 mile range, as well as combination walks of up to 23 miles.

Details of how to reach the starting points by car and where to park are given in the introductory information to each walk and any convenient railway stations are shown on the accompanying plan. As bus services are liable to frequent change, including information in this book might prove more misleading than helpful and so those wishing to reach the walks by bus are advised to obtain up-to-date information from the following hotlines:-

Bedfordshire/Luton   : Telephone : 0345-788788
Buckinghamshire   : Telephone : 0345-382000
Hertfordshire   : Telephone : 0345-244344

All the walks described here follow public rights of way, use recognised permissive paths or cross public open space. As the majority of walks cross land used for economic purposes such as agriculture, forestry or the rearing of game, walkers are urged to follow the Country Code at all times (see page 10). Observing these rules helps prevent financial loss to landowners and damage to the environment, as well as the all-too-frequent and sometimes justified bad feeling towards walkers in the countryside.

While it is hoped that the special maps provided with each walk will assist the user to complete the walks without going astray and skeleton details of the surrounding road network are given to enable walkers to shorten the routes in emergency, it is always advisable to take an Ordnance Survey or Chiltern Society map with you to enable you to shorten or otherwise vary the routes without using roads or get your bearings if you do become seriously lost. Details of the appropriate maps are given in the introductory information of each walk.

As for other equipment, readers are advised that some mud will normally be encountered on most walks particularly in woodland except in the driest weather. However proper walking boots are to be recommended at all times as, even when there are no mud problems, hard ruts or rough surfaces make the protection given by boots to the ankles desirable. In addition, the nature of the countryside makes many Chiltern paths prone to overgrowth, particularly in summer. To avoid resultant discomfort, protective clothing is advisable, especially where specific warnings are given.

In order to assist in coordinating the plans and the texts, all the numbers of path used have been shown on the plans and incorporated into the texts. These numbers, which are also shown on the Chiltern Society's series of footpath maps, consist of the official County Council footpath number with prefix letters used to indicate the parish concerned. It is therefore most helpful to use these when reporting any path problems you may find, together, if possible, with the national grid reference for the precise location of the trouble spot, as, in this way, the problem can be identified on the ground with a minimum of time loss in looking for it. National grid references can, however, only be calculated with the help of Ordnance Survey Landranger, Explorer or Pathfinder maps and an explanation of how this is done can be found in the Key to all Landranger and Explorer maps.

The length of time required for any particular walk depends on a number of factors such as your personal walking speed, the number of hills, stiles, etc. to be negotiated, whether or not you stop to rest, eat or drink, investigate places of interest, for children to play, etc. and the number of impediments such as mud, crops, overgrowth, ploughing, etc. which you encounter, but generally an average speed of between two and two and a half miles per hour (or perhaps one and a half miles per hour with young children) is about right in the Chilterns. It is, however, always advisable to allow extra time if you are limited by the daylight or catching a particular bus or train home in order to avoid your walk developing into a race against the clock.

Should you have problems with any of the paths used on the walks or find that the description given is no longer correct, the author would be most grateful if you could let him have details (c/o The Book Castle), so that attempts can be made to rectify the problem or the text can be corrected at the next reprint. Nevertheless, the author hopes that you will not encounter any serious problems and have pleasure from following the walks.

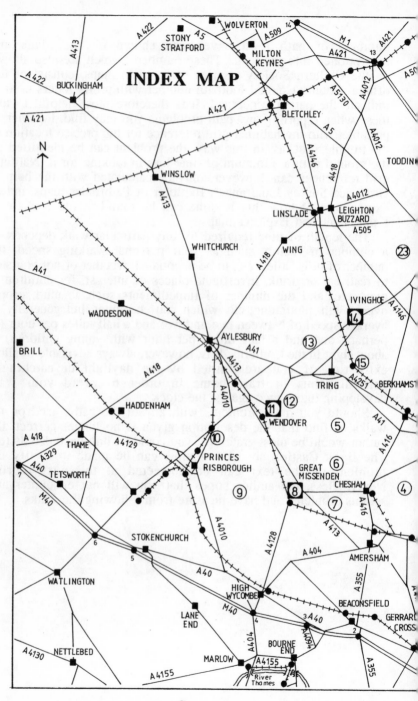

INDEX MAP

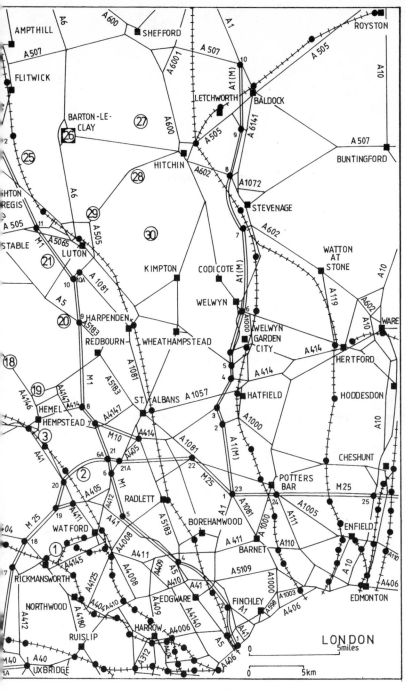

AMPTHILL

A6

A600

SHEFFORD

A1

ROYSTON

A507

A507

A505

A6001

10

A10

FLITWICK

A1(M)

LETCHWORTH

BALDOCK

BARTON-LE-CLAY

26

27

A600

9

A6141

A507

BUNTINGFORD

25

HITCHIN

A505

8

28

A602

A1072

HTON REGIS

A6

29

A505

STEVENAGE

7

A602

WATTON AT STONE

A10

STABLE

A505

11

A5065

M1

LUTON

30

21

KIMPTON

CODICOTE

A1(M)

A119

A10

10

10A

A1081

WELWYN

6

A602

WARE

A5

HARPENDEN

9

WELWYN GARDEN CITY

A1000

A10

20

A5183

REDBOURN

WHEATHAMPSTEAD

A414

HERTFORD

18

A1081

5

A414

HODDESDON

19

M1

A5183

ST. ALBANS

A1057

HATFIELD

4

A10

A4146

A4147

A414

HEMEL

8

3

A1081

A1000

CHESHUNT

HEMPSTEAD

7

2

A1(M)

A41

M10

A414

3

POTTERS BAR

M25

3

6A

21

A405

22

23

1

M25

2

6

21A

M1

RADLETT

24

A1005

25

A41

20

A405

A412

A5183

BOREHAMWOOD

A1081

A1000

A411

ENFIELD

19

M25

A41

5

A411

A110

WATFORD

A4008

4

BARNET

A10

A110

1

18

A4145

A411

A5109

A406

RICKMANSWORTH

A4125

A4008

A5

A41

A1000

A1003

EDMONTON

NORTHWOOD

A404

A410

EDGWARE

A410

A41

FINCHLEY

A598

A406

A412

A4180

A409

A4140

A1

A406

RUISLIP

HARROW

A4006

A5

LONDON

M40

A40

A312

5 miles

1A

UXBRIDGE

0   5km

9

Country Code

- Guard against all risk of fire

- Fasten all gates

- Keep dogs under proper control

- Keep to the paths across farmland

- Avoid damaging fences, hedges and walls

- Leave no litter - take it home

- Safeguard water supplies

- Protect wild life, wild plants and trees

- Go carefully on country roads on the right-hand side facing oncoming traffic

- Respect the life of the countryside

WALK 1   Croxley Green

Length of Walk: 5.3 miles / 8.6 Km
Starting Point: Mini-roundabout by Croxley Green Church and the 'Sportsman'.
Grid Ref: TQ069953
Maps: OS Landranger Sheets 166 or 176
OS Pathfinder Sheet 1139 (TQ09/19)
How to get there / Parking: Croxley Green, 0.8 miles north-east of the centre of Rickmansworth, may be reached from the town by taking the A412 towards Watford. At the mini-roundabout by Croxley Green Church and the 'Sportsman' fork left onto the Sarratt road where there are parking bays on your left or you can park in nearby side-streets.

Croxley Green, on a hilltop between the Chess and Gade valleys and Rickmansworth and Watford, was till the early twentieth century a small village built around an extensive green, but the coming of the railways followed by the inter-war 'Metroland' house-building boom led to a rapid expansion of Croxley Green and the neighbouring towns which completely eroded the gaps between them. Luckily for Croxley Green, however, the village green survived and the coming of the Green Belt prevented development to the north while the Gade and Colne valleys to the south were too wet for development. Thus not only do attractive rural walks from this suburban settlement remain possible, but the fine green also preserves something of its traditional village atmosphere. While Croxley Green was historically a hamlet of Rickmansworth and so did not have its own church and become a separate ecclesiastical parish till 1872 and only became a separate civil parish in 1986, the church is unusual in having a circular tower and Croxley Hall Farm has a farmhouse dating in part from the sixteenth century and a weatherboarded mediaeval aisled tithe barn with a tiled kingpost roof built by St. Albans Abbey in the 1390s and believed to be the second largest in England.

The walk first takes you the length of the village green before exploring the heavily-wooded countryside to the north and reaching the Grand Union Canal towpath in Cassiobury Park on

11

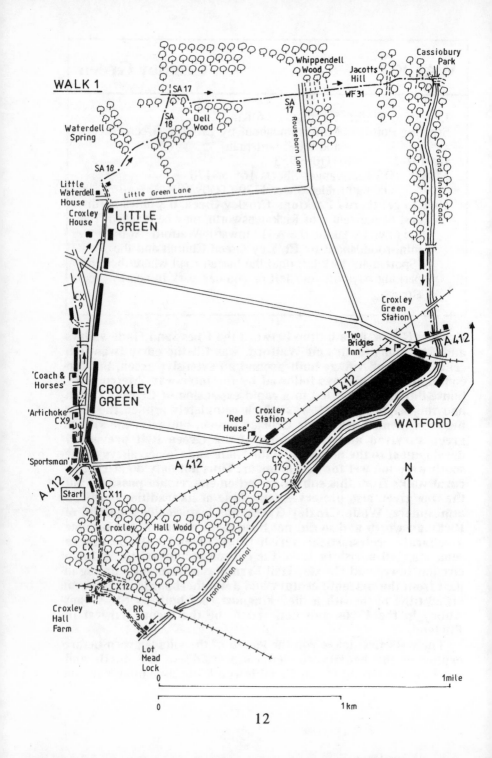

WALK 1

Cassiobury Park

Whippendell Wood

Jacotts Hill

SA 17

WF 31

SA 17

SA 17

SA 18

Dell Wood

Waterdell Spring

Grand Union Canal

Rousebarn Lane

SA 18

Little Waterdell House

Little Green Lane

Croxley House

LITTLE GREEN

CX 9

Croxley Green Station

'Two Bridges Inn'

A 412

'Coach & Horses'

CROXLEY GREEN

WATFORD

'Artichoke' CX9

'Red House'

Croxley Station

'Sportsman'

A 412

CX 17

N

Start

CX 11

A 412

Croxley Hall Wood

CX 11

Croxley Hall Farm

CX 12

RK 30

Grand Union Canal

Lot Mead Lock

0   1mile

0   1km

the edge of Watford. You then follow this tranquil and in parts very attractive waterway for over two miles around the eastern and southern periphery of Croxley Green before returning by way of the historic Croxley Hall Farm to the village centre.

Starting from the mini-roundabout by Croxley Green Church and the ´Sportsman`, take the left-hand pavement of The Green, signposted to Sarratt, crossing Windmill Drive, then take path CX9, a gravel path gradually diverging from the road, straight on along the back of the green passing the war memorial, the ´Artichoke` and the ´Coach and Horses`. Now keep left at a fork crossing Copthorne Road and continuing along the back of the green with views of Croxley House (now a WRVS residential care home) ahead. Having passed two seats, by a signposted path to your left, bear half right across the green heading for the corner of a wall left of some white railings in its far corner, crossing two roads and passing left of a pond to reach a third.

Turn left down this quiet lane and where it forks by attractive brick-and-timber cottages at Little Green, bear slightly left onto path SA18 taking the drive to Little Waterdell House past the house to Coachman´s Cottage. Here take a narrow fenced path straight on to a kissing-gate into a field then turn right and follow a right-hand hedge, later a fence, to cross a stile by the corner of a wood called Waterdell Spring. Now follow the edge of the wood straight on to cross a further stile, then a right-hand fence to a stile at the corner of Dell Wood. Do **NOT** cross this stile, but bear half left across the field to a stile into a wood called Round Newland´s Spring, through which you continue to a fence gap into the corner of a field. Here turn right onto path SA17, ignoring a stile back into the wood and following the outside edge of the wood bearing right and then left to cross a stile in the next hedge. Now go straight on downhill across the next field to a hedge gap with an old kissing-gate frame leading to Rousebarn Lane.

Cross this road to enter Whippendell Wood, part of the ancient Cassiobury Park set out in 1545 by Sir Richard Morrison who built the first of a series of three great houses of the same name, which from the seventeenth century to 1922 were the home of the Earls of Essex. Unfortunately the last of these houses, designed by the architect of Ashridge, James Wyatt in 1800, was demolished in 1927 to make way for a Watford housing estate and what was left of the park was, in part, converted into a golf course interspersed with woodland and, in part, became a public park for Watford. Now take path WF31 straight on uphill through the wood, ignoring five crossing paths and emerging onto the West Herts Golf Course at the top of Jacotts Hill. Here go straight on across two fairways, looking out for balls being driven from the right and then the left, and passing between two tees to enter more woodland. Disregard a crossing track, then, on emerging onto another fairway where balls are driven from your right, keep straight on, entering further woodland, ignoring a crossing path by a tee and descending to a junction of tracks near a bridge over the Grand Union Canal into the modern Cassiobury Park.

Here bear half right down some steps onto the towpath of this two-hundred-year-old canal, then turn right and follow it for two and a quarter miles in a quiet wooded setting at first, then passing under a series of four bridges near Croxley Green Station where a lock and marina make things busier. You then continue along a quieter tree-lined section passing Croxley papermills, established in 1830, before reaching a lock where you fork left under a low bridge and continue for a further two-thirds of a mile. Having passed under another railway bridge carrying the Metropolitan Line, at the beginning of Lot Mead Lock, turn right down a concrete ramp onto path RK30, passing through white gates and taking a stony track along the edge of a field and past a car park, then bearing left to reach a gate by Croxley Hall Farm. Go through this gate and turn right onto path CX12, crossing a railway bridge and bearing right along a rough lane through Croxley Hall Wood. Where the lane forks, turn sharp left onto path CX11, then at a second fork bear right and continue for a third of a mile, leaving Croxley Hall Wood and reaching the A412 where your starting point is to your left.

WALK 2   Abbot´s Langley

Length of Walk: 4.5 miles / 7.3 Km
Starting Point: Entrance to public car park in Abbot´s
                    Langley High Street.
Grid Ref: TL094019
Maps: OS Landranger Sheet 166
            OS Pathfinder Sheet 1119 (TL00/10)
How to get there / Parking: Abbot´s Langley, 3 miles north
    of the centre of Watford, may be reached by leaving the
    M25 at Junction 20 (Hunton Bridge) and taking the
    A4251 towards King´s Langley. At the next roundabout
    turn right towards Home Park Industrial Estate, then, at a
    T-junction, turn right passing King´s Langley Station then
    under the M25. After a narrow railway bridge controlled
    by traffic lights, take the second turning left (Gallowshill
    Lane) and follow it uphill for three-quarters of a mile to
    reach a signposted free car park on the left in the centre
    of the village.

Although the village of Abbot´s Langley is today rather
swamped by suburban housing development, its centre on a hilltop above the Gade valley has retained its old-world rural
charm. Abbot´s Langley can, indeed, boast an interesting church
with a Norman tower and arcades but a later exterior with a fine
stuccoed Georgian vicarage nearby. The first part of its name
derives from the manor being held from Saxon times till the
Dissolution by the abbots of St. Albans and differentiates it from
its neighbour King´s Langley where there was a mediæval royal
palace. After its confiscation by the Crown the manor was held in
the seventeenth century by William and Elizabeth Greenhill who
conceived the record number of no less than 39 children (32
daughters and 7 sons), all of whom survived to adulthood. It is
even said that Elizabeth thought she could have had two or three
more if her husband had not died while she was expecting her
thirty-ninth child! In the early twentieth century, following the
opening of the Ovaltine factory in the Gade valley below, two
model farms were constructed north of the village to supply the
ingredients, both with half-timbered thatched buildings but, when
the M25 was built through their farmland, the farms were sold

15

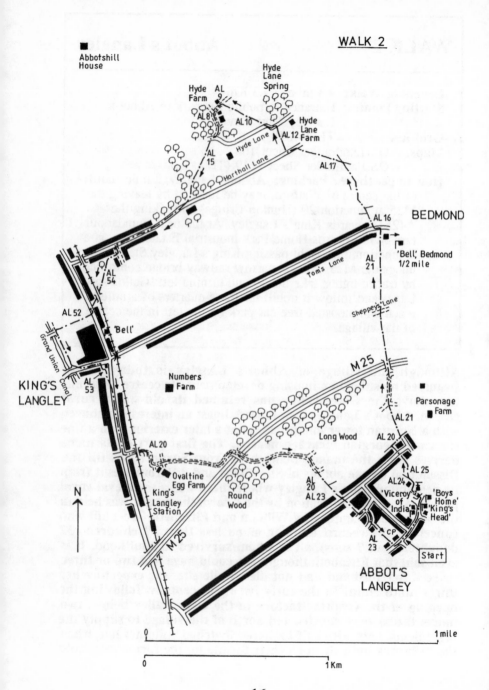

Abbotshill
House

Hyde
Lane
Spring

Hyde
Farm   AL
        9

AL 8

AL 10   Hyde
         Lane
         Farm

AL 12

AL
15   Hyde Lane

Horthall Lane

AL 17

AL 16

BEDMOND

'Bell', Bedmond
1/2 mile

AL
21

Tom's Lane

Sheppey's Lane

AL 54

AL 52

Grand Union Canal

'Bell'

KING'S
LANGLEY

AL
53

Numbers
Farm

M 25

Parsonage
Farm

AL 21

Long Wood

AL 20

AL 20

AL 20

Ovaltine
Egg Farm

King's
Langley
Station

Round
Wood

AL
20
AL 23

AL 25

AL 24

'Viceroy
of India'

'Boys'
Home'
'King's
Head'

CP

AL
23

Start

N

M 25

ABBOT'S
LANGLEY

0   1 mile

0   1 Km

16

and became disused. The former Ovaltine Dairy Farm has since been converted into private dwellings known as Antoinette Court recalling the fact that it was modelled on the dairy built for Marie Antoinette at Versailles.

The walk soon leaves Abbot's Langley behind and crosses the M25 to explore the surprisingly remote hillside to the north of the village separating Abbot's Langley from Hemel Hempstead with fine views across the Gade valley in places. Eventually you drop into the valley on the edge of King's Langley briefly joining the Grand Union Canal towpath and passing the Ovaltine factory before climbing past the former Ovaltine Egg Farm to return to Abbot's Langley.

Starting from the entrance to the car park in Abbot's Langley High Street, turn left along the High Street for some 250 yards to reach a lychgate leading to the church. Here turn left onto path AL24 along a macadam drive left of the lychgate passing left of the church. By the vicarage bear right into the churchyard, where you turn left and then fork right onto path AL25 passing through an avenue of lime trees. At the far corner of the churchyard go through a gate into an alleyway, soon crossing Parsonage Close and continuing to the edge of a field. Here turn right onto fenced path AL20 then at the corner of the field turn left onto fenced path AL21. After the enclosing fence peters out, follow a right-hand hedge then a fence straight on to a stile onto a farm road. Cross the farm road and a stile opposite and take a wide track straight on with views towards King's Langley to your left to reach a stile leading to a footbridge over the M25. At the far end of the bridge cross a stile and take what is normally a crop-break straight on downhill joining a left-hand fence and reaching a crossing bridleway called Sheppey's Lane in the bottom of the dip. Now bear slightly right heading for the left-hand of two tall poplars in the top hedge where you cross a stile and take a fenced path to reach Tom's Lane at Bedmond.

Bedmond, the centre of which is on the hilltop to your right, was in about 1100 the birthplace of Nicholas Breakspear, the only Englishman ever to become Pope. His papacy as Adrian IV from 1154 to 1159 was short but significant as it was he who approved Henry II's request for permission to conquer Ireland and he who ordered the execution of Arnold of Brescia. He also took on Holy Roman Emperor Frederick Barbarossa, whom he was about to excommunicate when he suddenly died possibly due to poisoning. A former local inn called the 'Travellers' Rest' is also said to have been a haunt of the highwayman Dick Turpin who would hide there in a spacious chimney when sought by the local justices.

Turn left into Tom's Lane then after 40 yards turn right through a squeeze-stile onto enclosed path AL16. At the back of gardens to your left, disregard a branching path to your left and go straight on through a squeeze-stile into a field. Now follow a right-hand hedge straight on ignoring a branching path to your right. At the far side of the field go straight on through a squeeze-stile and bear slightly left across the next field aiming just right of Hyde Lane Farm. On reaching a midfield cattle trough, bear half left onto crossing path AL17, heading for the left-hand of two copses on the skyline to reach a stile into Harthall Lane. Turn left onto this road, then, after 40 yards, turn right over a stile onto path AL12 following a right-hand hedge across a field to a stile into Hyde Lane. Turn left onto this road and follow it round a sharp right-hand bend, then at a sharp left-hand bend turn right over a stile onto path AL10 bearing half left across the field heading for a clump of ash trees right of a gap in the far hedge. Here cross a stile then follow the hedge to cross a stile by a gate in the hedge gap where a fine view opens out ahead towards Abbotshill House, built in 1839 by the paper manufacturer, John Dickinson and now a school, Hemel Hempstead and the woods of distant Ashridge Park.

Now turn left onto a farm road (path AL9) passing through Hyde Farm, bearing left to pass right of a green barn and, now on path AL8, continuing through white gates where you bear slightly right to reach a bend in Hyde Lane. Turn right onto this road, then almost immediately left over a stile onto path AL15 following a left-hand fence to cross a stile then bearing half right across two more fields to cross a concealed stile right of a tall oak tree into a copse. In the copse bear left and follow an obvious winding path to reach Harthall Lane by a redundant stile step. Turn right onto this road and follow it downhill for a quarter mile, soon with houses on both sides. Opposite house no.17 on the right, turn left onto path AL54 taking a macadam lane uphill which soon loses its surface. At the back of the right-hand gardens turn right onto a fenced path, soon with a field to your left, then continue through a low railway subway (tall walkers should mind their heads!) and bear left between garden fences to reach a road called Primrose Hill on the edge of King's Langley.

King's Langley, which, strictly speaking, is on the other side of the River Gade, had a mediæval royal palace and priory on a hill above the village, but the palace declined following a fire in the fifteenth century while the priory fell victim to the Dissolution so that nothing now remains of the palace while remnants of the priory are incorporated into the Rudolf Steiner School. The priory was the original burial place of both Richard II and Prince Edmund de Langley, the first Duke of York, but while Richard II´s remains were moved to Westminster Abbey, Edmund de Langley now lies in the fifteenth-century parish church.

Cross Primrose Hill and turn left along its far pavement, then, after 40 yards, turn right past a barrier onto macadam path AL52 following the edge of a recreation ground to reach the Grand Union Canal towpath. Here ignore steps leading to a footbridge and turn left onto the towpath passing a lock. On nearing a road bridge, turn left along a gravel path leading to Water Lane, then continue along it. Some 50 yards short of a T-junction turn right onto fenced path AL53 and follow it to Station Road. Turn right onto this road and follow it for a quarter mile passing the Ovaltine factory, now part of the Swiss Sandoz concern, then opposite Roman Gardens turn left onto a road passing under the railway. Now ignore a branching track to your left and take the left-hand of two roads branching to your right. Now on path AL20, follow this road uphill, bearing left by the former Ovaltine Egg Farm with a view to your left towards Numbers Farm with its timber-framed farmhouse and weatherboarded barn with a timber-framed gable end. On nearing the M25, where the road bears left again, there are fine views to your left towards the Ovaltine factory, King´s Langley and Hemel Hempstead.

Now continue over the M25 and bear left ignoring a branching drive and a farm track to your right. Where the track forks by an old iron gate, bear half right onto a track across a field, then, where this track turns left, leave it and follow a sporadic right-hand hedge straight on to reach a thick hedge at the edge of Abbot´s Langley. Here ignore a branching path to your left and take fenced path AL23 straight on to reach Abbots Road. Cross this road and go straight on along an alleyway to another road called Dell Meadow. Having crossed this, bear half left along the pavement of Standfield which bears right. Now turn left into an alleyway between nos. 13 and 15 passing the car park to reach the High Street near your starting point.

WALK 3   Hemel Hempstead (Apsley)

Length of Walk: 4.8 miles / 7.8 Km
Starting Point: Roundabout by Apsley Church.
Grid Ref: TL060051
Maps: OS Landranger Sheet 166
             OS Pathfinder Sheet 1119 (TL00/10)
             Chiltern Society FP Map No.5
How to get there / Parking: Apsley, 1 mile southeast of the
             centre of Hemel Hempstead, may be reached from
             the junction of the A414 and A4251 at Two Waters
             by taking the A4251 towards King´s Langley for
             half a mile. Just before reaching Apsley Church, turn
             right into Kents Avenue and park here or in one of
             the nearby side-streets. Alternatively there is a public
             car park nearer to Two Waters.

Apsley, in the Gade valley on the southern edge of Hemel Hempstead, where some of the nineteenth-century papermills have
recently given way to a modern supermarket and factories, may
appear from the A4251 to be an unpromising location to start a
Chiltern walk. There is, however, open country less than 100
yards away, south of the railway and the towpath of the Grand
Union Canal, whose construction in the 1790s made Apsley
attractive for the paper manufacturers, now provides a surprisingly quiet and green corridor through the town leading to Heath
Park and branching paths into the country. Despite its origins in
the industrial revolution, Apsley is also a place of historic interest
as, following the purchase of several papermills by the London
stationer, John Dickinson in the early nineteenth century, it was
here that he developed the recent discovery of how to produce
paper in a continuous sheet in order to enable modern mass
newspaper production and his mills also supplied some of the
high-quality paper used in producing early postage stamps.
    The walk soon leads you to the Grand Union Canal towpath
which it follows to Heath Park before you turn south and climb to
a surprisingly quiet and remote hilltop plateau near Chipperfield
with wide views across the surrounding hills and Gade valley
before passing through Shendish Park and dropping into Apsley.

Starting from the roundabout by Apsley Church, take the A4251 towards Hemel Hempstead. At its junction with Kents Avenue turn right onto path HH71 down the side of Sainsbury´s to the bank of the River Gade. Here turn right beside the river to reach a foot-bridge over the confluence of the Gade and the Grand Union Canal. At the far end of the bridge turn left down some steps onto the canal towpath and follow it to bridge no.153, an original hump-backed bridge over the canal from the 1790s. Turn left over this bridge and then right continuing along the towpath. At a road bridge by the ´Albion`, go straight on under it with the previous industrial scene giving way to parkland. Now keep straight on, soon with a view of the Kodak headquarters ahead which dominate the Hemel Hempstead skyline, crossing a bridge over a weir on the Gade and soon passing under the A414 road bridge into Heath Park. Here look out for the remains of the bridge piers of the barely perceptible ´Nicky Line`, an old Midland Railway branch from Harpenden to Hemel Hempstead whose course is marked by lines of willows and pollarded chestnut trees. Continue past a lock ignoring a stile to your left and crossing a bridge over a weir. 200 yards further on, turn left over a stile in the hedge and take path HH79 bearing slightly left along a raised path across a water-meadow to reach a footbridge over the River Bulbourne. At the far end of this bridge, fork right onto raised path HH77 following a right-hand hedge to a kissing-gate onto the A4251 at Two Waters.

Bear slightly right across this road and take fenced path HH76 between two sets of gates into the gasworks, soon crossing a high footbridge over part of the gasworks site then descending steps into the former Nicky Line cutting. At the far side of the cutting climb some steps and go through a belt of scrub to a bridge over the main Euston (or old L&NWR) line built by Robert Stephenson in 1838, then climb more steps and bear left to a kissing-gate into a field. Follow a left-hand hedge straight on uphill with views across Hemel Hempstead opening out behind you. At the top of the field ignore a branching path to your right, go straight on through a kissing-gate and follow the left-hand hedge over the hill and down to a kissing-gate onto the A414. Here turn right, crossing a slip-road and passing under the A41 bridge, then cross another slip-road and take path HH75 straight on up a flight of steps. At the top bear half left through a plantation to reach a kissing-gate into Featherbed Lane. Turn left onto this road and follow it for some 300 yards with fine views to your left across Hemel Hempstead.

At a sharp bend where the road bears left to a bridge over the A41, turn right onto byway HH72, following a pleasant stony lane for three-quarters of a mile, passing through Great Wood and eventually emerging onto Rucklers Lane. Turn right onto this narrow road with wide views and follow it for 200 yards to a road junction. Here turn left into Barnes Lane and follow this quiet country lane with panoramic views across the plateau for half a mile rounding a sharp left-hand bend by the corner of Badger Dell Wood and later rounding a right-hand and another left-hand bend. 100 yards beyond the second left-hand bend, turn left over a stile onto crossing path KL19 bearing slightly right and heading for the left-hand end of Dark Wood in the next dip. On reaching a clump of trees, follow its edge straight on downhill to join the A41 fence leading to a kissing-gate and steps down into Rucklers Lane.

Turn right onto this road passing under the A41, then disregard a concrete drive to your left and turn left onto the continuation of path KL19 taking the right-hand of two drives steeply uphill. Ignore a branching drive to your right, then, near the top of the hill where the drive forks, take a woodland path straight on to a stile into a field. Go straight on across this field aiming for a beech tree whose trunk is not hidden by branches in the tree belt surrounding the grounds of Shendish Manor, with views across the Gade valley to your right towards Abbotshill House, built by John Dickinson in 1839 and now a school. On reaching the tree belt, turn right and follow its edge to a three-armed signpost.

Now take path KL17 straight on beside the tree belt, soon with a fence to your right and with glimpses of Shendish Manor through the trees to your left, crossing a stile, the main drive to Shendish Manor and a strip of grass to join a branching drive. Take this drive straight on, bearing left by green gates then keeping right at a fork to reach a belt of trees by a green wooden building. At the far side of the tree belt turn right onto a crossing drive passing some farm cottages and a bungalow and entering Hen's Head Wood. In the wood ignore a branching golfers' path to your left, then at a Y-fork bear right onto a drive which descends gently. Where the drive bears left, leave it, going straight on past a green barrier then through gates onto a parkland golf course. Here bear slightly left, passing left of a large cedar. At a signposted path junction take worn path KL18 straight on downhill passing through a clump of tall lime trees and continuing to a tall Scots pine tree at the bottom edge of the golf course. Now go straight on through a tree belt to a footbridge over the main railway line. At the far end of the bridge descend several flights of steps then take macadam path HH74 bearing left through Apsley churchyard to reach the church where you turn right and right again for your starting point.

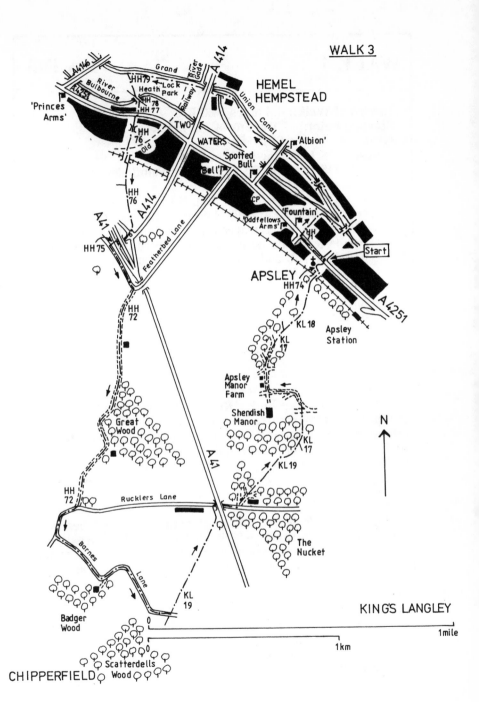

WALK 3

'Princes Arms'

HEMEL HEMPSTEAD

Grand
River Bulbourne
Lock
Heath Park
HH 79
HH 78
HH 77

River Gade
A 414
Railway
Union Canal

TWO
WATERS

'Albion'
'Spotted Bull'
Bell'
HH 76
Old
HH 76
A 414
A 41
HH 75

CP
Fountain
'Oddfellows Arms'
HH
Start
A 4251

APSLEY
HH 74
KL 18
KL 17
Apsley Station

Featherbed Lane
HH 72

KL 17
Apsley Manor Farm
Shendish Manor

N

Great Wood
KL 17
KL 19

HH 72
Rucklers Lane
The Nucket
A 41

Barnes Lane
KL 19

Badger Wood

KING'S LANGLEY

0   1mile

0   1km

CHIPPERFIELD
Scatterdells Wood

23

WALK 4   Ley Hill

Length of Walk: 4.3 miles / 7.0 Km
Starting Point: `The Crown`, Ley Hill.
Grid Ref: SP990019
Maps: OS Landranger Sheet 165
       OS Explorer Sheet 2 (or old Pathfinder Sheet 1118 (SP80/90))
       Chiltern Society FP Map No.17
How to get there / Parking: Ley Hill, 2 miles east of Chesham, may be reached from the town by following the signposted route from the northern end of the town centre up White Hill and then turning right at a mini-roundabout into Botley Road and keeping straight on for 1.4 miles. At a multiple road junction by `The Crown` and `The Swan`, turn right and park either in a small car park on the left on the common or in the loop road in front of the pubs.

Ley Hill, although connected to Chesham by a continuous ribbon of development along Botley Road, remains very much a typical hilltop Buckinghamshire Chiltern hamlet with its pubs and cottages scattered around its extensive common. Presumably as a result of modern motor traffic, the common, which extends to the Hertfordshire boundary, has long since ceased to be grazed by sheep and so where it has not been converted for use as a golf course or cricket field, scrub and even woodland have taken over.

The walk explores the hilltop plateau above the Chess Valley to the east of Chesham, which, despite its close proximity to London and Chesham, retains a surprising air of remoteness and totally belies the fact of being less than 25 miles from Central London. It first takes you westwards through woodland to the hamlet of Tyler's Hill before fine views open out and you cross a deep Chiltern bottom to reach Hill Farm near the edge of Chesham. You then turn eastwards with more fine views recrossing the bottom and taking an ancient green lane to White End Park. Just beyond this in Codmore Wood you turn north, eventually crossing Ley Hill Common to reach your starting point.

Starting with your back to the 'Crown' and the 'Swan' at Ley Hill, turn left along the loop road crossing the entrance to Kiln Lane, then bear half left across the grass to join a stony track. Follow this past the Methodist Church and a bungalow called 'Homelee'. Now turn left into narrow enclosed path LT17, soon passing the end of a cul-de-sac road and continuing to a stile into a field. Here turn right and follow the edge of a copse then a right-hand hedge to cross a stile into Cowcroft Wood. In the wood go straight on, then, where the right-hand field gives way to woodland, fork right by a tree with two trunks onto a narrow path, turning right at a T-junction. By the corner of a field ahead turn left onto a waymarked path ignoring all branching paths to your left. At a fork by two Y-shaped trees, bear right and at a second fork, bear left onto path LT17a to cross a stile into a field. Here turn left onto path CM131 following the outside edge of the wood towards the red-brick church at Tyler's Hill to a corner of the field where you turn right. Now cross a stile by the first of a line of three tall cypress trees and take a fenced path joining a drive and reaching Tyler's Hill Road at Tyler's Hill opposite the 'Five Bells'.

Cross this road and a stile by a gate opposite and take path CM49a straight on, passing just left of a cattle trough to cross a stile in the far corner of the field. Here take path CM49 following a left-hand hedge, later a fence, straight on, ignoring a branching path to your right and then continuing with fine views ahead towards the Chess Valley and Chesham Bois hidden in trees on the skyline and eventually descending to reach a hedge gap into Bottom Lane (bridleway CM28) in the valley bottom. Turn right into this lane then immediately left onto sunken bridleway CM54 following it uphill for 350 yards. At the top of the hill ignore a field gate to your left, then, where the lane widens out, turn left over a concealed stile onto path CM55. Now bear slightly left across a field passing left of two oak trees to cross a stile left of an oak tree in the far hedge, then follow a left-hand hedge downhill through two fields to a stile into Bottom Lane.

Cross this lane and a stile opposite then bear slightly right across a field corner to a stile into Green Lane (bridleway CM29). Turn left into this lane and follow it uphill to enter woodland where you ignore a branching path to your left and continue along the edge of the wood. On reaching a branching bridleway to your right, take bridleway LT18 straight on, leaving the wood, disregarding a branching bridleway to your left and following Green Lane straight on for a third of a mile to a gate by farm buildings. Now take a concrete road straight on to reach a public road opposite an outbuilding of White End Park.

Turn left onto this road, then, after 150 yards, turn right over a stile by tall gates onto path LT1 following a right-hand fence straight on with views to your right of White End Park with its palmhouse. At the far side of the field cross a stile, Blackwell Hall Lane and another stile opposite and go straight on across a field to a stile into Codmore Wood. In the wood go straight on, ignoring two crossing tracks and passing a pond to your right. On nearing the far edge of the wood, turn sharp left onto path LT4 and follow it to reach a wide track onto which you turn right. (NB If this part of path LT4 is impassably overgrown, retrace your steps to the nearer of the crossing tracks and turn right onto it to rejoin the correct line). Some 60 yards short of a gate onto Codmore Wood Road, turn left onto a waymarked path through the trees to a rail-stile onto the road. Turn left onto the road then almost immediately turn right through a hedge gap into a field and take path LT4 following a left-hand hedge gently downhill into a copse called Knotts Spring. On reaching a stile in the left-hand fence, turn left over this, cross a second stile and leaving the copse, follow a right-hand hedge uphill. Where the ground levels out, continue along the edge of another copse called Long Knotts to a stile leading to Blackwell Hall Lane at a road junction on the edge of Ley Hill Common.

Here turn sharp right onto a branching road and follow it uphill. At a right-hand bend by a flint cottage, turn left onto path LT14 crossing a golf course fairway (beware of balls being driven from your left!) and going through an obvious gap into a belt of scrub. In the scrub bear right at a fork passing between golf tees then, at successive forks, keep right and then left to emerge onto another fairway. Here turn left and follow the edge of the fairway to a road near your starting point.

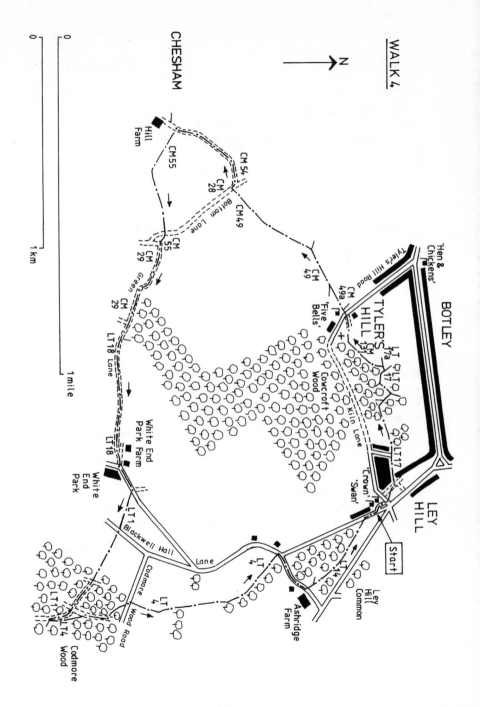

WALK 4

N

CHESHAM

BOTLEY

LEY HILL

TYLER'S HILL

'Hen & Chickens'

Tyler's Hill Road

'Five Bells'

Cowcroft Wood

Kiln Lane

'Crown'

'Swan'

Start

Ley Hill Common

LT 14

LT 1

Blackwell Hall Lane

Codmore

Wood Road

Ashridge Farm

LT 4

LT 4

Codmore Wood

LT 14

LT 18

White End Park

White End Park Farm

LT 18 Lane

CM 29

CM 29

Green Lane

CM 55

CM 55

CM 28

CM 54

Bottom Lane

CM 49

CM 49

CM 49a

LT 17

LT 17a

CM 31

LT 17

Hill Farm

0

0

1 km

1 mile

27

WALK 5   Cholesbury

Length of Walk: (A) 4.7 miles / 7.6 Km
                    (B) 2.8 miles / 4.5 Km
Starting Point: Cholesbury Village Hall.
Grid Ref: SP930071
Maps: OS Landranger Sheet 165
           OS Explorer Sheet 2 (or old Pathfinder Sheet 1118
           (SP80/90))
           Chiltern Society FP Map No.8
How to get there / Parking: Cholesbury, 4 miles northwest of
    Chesham, may be reached from the town by taking the
    A416 northwards. At a sharp right-hand bend, leave the
    A416 and continue straight on along a road signposted to
    Cholesbury and Hawridge (**not** Bellingdon) and follow it
    for 3.7 miles to Cholesbury Common. The village hall is
    on the right about 150 yards past a turning signposted to
    Tring. Cars can be parked along the edge of the common.

Cholesbury, with its cottages scattered around its spacious
ridgetop common, is one of the most unspoilt villages in the Bucks
Chilterns and forms the gateway to some of their most remote
country. The village is an ancient settlement, as its thirteenth-
century church, largely rebuilt in 1872-3, stands within a ten-
feet-high Iron Age camp enclosing fifteen acres of land and its
Saxon name of ´Ceolweald´s burh` confirms the camp existed at
that time. Originally a hilltop hamlet of Drayton Beauchamp,
whose mother village is 3.5 miles to the northwest in the Vale of
Aylesbury, following the construction of Cholesbury Church as a
chapel-of-ease, the village at some time became a separate
parish, which in 1934 was amalgamated with the neighbouring
parish of Hawridge and the remaining hilltop areas of the Vale
parishes of Drayton Beauchamp, Buckland and Aston Clinton to
form the modern hilltop parish of Cholesbury-cum-St. Leonards.
    Both walks explore the heavily-wooded remote plateau to the
north of Cholesbury passing through the Iron Age camp and
crossing the back of the common before entering Hertfordshire
and crossing a ridge between two incipient Chiltern bottoms to
reach Tring Grange. Here you turn north to enter woodland,
through which Walk B returns direct to Cholesbury, while Walk

A heads northwestwards towards Hastoe, the highest village in Hertfordshire to follow a section of Grim´s Ditch before returning via Buckland Common to Cholesbury.

Both walks start from Cholesbury Village Hall and take path CY26 over a stile by a gate at the left-hand end of the hall and along a rough lane to cross a stile by a gate and a black wooden shed. Now turn right onto path CY23 passing the shed then bearing slightly right to cross a stile in a field corner. A few yards further on, turn right over a stile into a belt of woodland sheltering the earthworks of the camp. Follow a path along the top of its left-hand mound to a crossing cattle track where the ditch and mounds have been levelled. Here turn right into the middle of the ditch then bear half left through a gap between hollybushes and immediately fork right onto path CY23a passing right of some overgrown rails and following a right-hand fence through scrub to reach Shire Lane, so called because much of it forms the county boundary with Hertfordshire.

Turn left onto this road. Just before a gravel drive to your left, turn sharp right onto path CY48r ignoring a track to a gate and taking a grassy track doubling back across a wooded part of the common to a gravel drive by a house onto which you turn right to reach another road. Cross this and take path CY48j straight on along a grassy track, ignoring branching paths to your right. Where the main track bears right, take a lesser path straight on through the bushes bearing left to a stile into a field at the county boundary. Now take path TU5 bearing right across the field to a gate and stile in its top fence, then bear half right across a second field crossing a stile and continuing to a stile just left of the far corner of the third. Here follow a right-hand fence downhill to a gate and stile, then take a grassy track beside a left-hand fence and sporadic hedge towards Tring Grange, later with a fence to your right and the track becoming surfaced. Having passed the house and stables, at a track junction turn left onto bridleway TU3, a stony track gently ascending the valley bottom for nearly half a mile, to reach a road.

Cross this road and a stile opposite into a wood, then take path TU10, keeping left at a fork and bearing left then right to join a left-hand mossy bank which you follow along an avenue of oaks and beeches for 400 yards to a gate and rails into a field. Do **NOT** cross the rails but turn left onto path TU9 passing left of the rails then bearing left deeper into Roundhill Wood where it soon widens into a timber track. On nearing a gate, fork left off the track to cross a stile onto a road. Cross the road and a stile opposite and take path TU12 straight on for 300 yards through a wood called

High Scrubs to a stile onto a wide crossing track (byway TU77), onto which **Walk A** turns right. Now omit the next paragraph.

Walk B crosses the track and takes path TU12 straight on to leave the wood by a stile and follow a left-hand hedge to a stile into Shire Lane opposite a cottage. Turn left onto this road then immediately right over a stile onto fenced path CY27 along the edge of Drayton Wood, whose name reminds us of the ancient link with Drayton Beauchamp. On crossing a stile into the wood, continue along its inside edge to the far end of the left-hand field then turn left over a stile onto path CY26 following a right-hand hedge to a stile into Tomlin's Wood. Keep straight on through the wood eventually crossing another stile and soon emerging into open scrub. Ignore a branching track to your right and continue through a gap in the tree-belt sheltering Cholesbury's Iron Age camp to cross a stile by a gate. Now bear slightly right following a grassy track across a paddock, with a view of the church to your right, to cross wooden rails by a gate, then continue through another paddock to a gate and stile by a black shed where you retrace your outward route to your starting point.

Walk A continues on byway TU77 for nearly a mile, ignoring a crossing path, eventually leaving the wood and proceeding along a green lane. At the end of a tree-belt to your left sheltering part of the Iron Age earthwork called Grim's Ditch, turn left through a hedge gap onto path TU14 along the left-hand edge of the tree-belt to the far end of the field. Here turn left onto path TU16 following a right-hand hedge. Where the hedge turns right, bear half right across the field to a gap into the near corner of a copse. Take the obvious path straight on through the copse to a stile into Shire Lane.

Cross this road and a stile opposite and take path CY25a straight across a field to a gate and stile into Drayton Wood, whose name reminds us of the ancient link with Drayton Beauchamp. Go straight on through the wood with rhododendron bushes to your left, after 100 yards keeping left at a fork and still skirting the rhododendrons. At a second fork go right onto path CY40a, soon bearing left at an unmarked fork to reach a stile out of the wood. Now follow a left-hand fence downhill and up again past Beechwood Farm to your left to a stile into a second field, then continue beside a left-hand hedge. 40 yards beyond a large oak tree ignore a hedge gap to your left then turn left over a stile onto path CY40 following a left-hand hedge to a stile into a rough lane (path CY20). Turn left into this lane to reach Little Twye Road, then take path CY14 straight on over a stile bearing slightly right

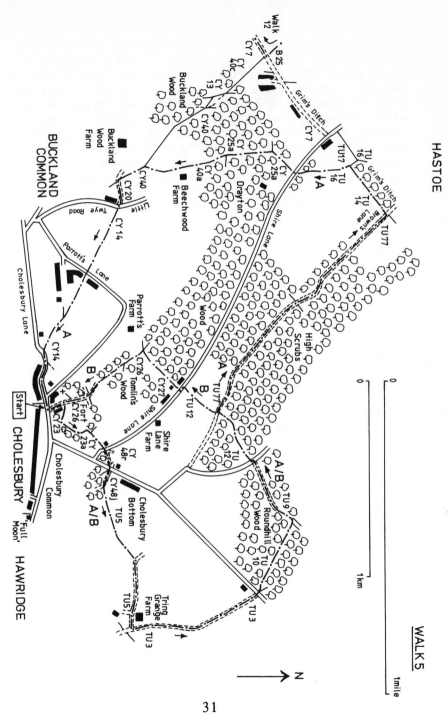

HASTOE

WALK 5

BUCKLAND COMMON

HAWRIDGE

CHOLESBURY

Start

'Full Moon'

Cholesbury Common

Cholesbury Lane

Parrott's Lane

Twye Road

Little Twye Road

BUCKLAND COMMON

Buckland Wood Farm

Buckland Wood

Walk 12

B 25

Grim's Ditch

Grim's Ditch

Brown's Lane

CY 7

CY 7

CY 40c

CY 13

CY 40

CY 25a

CY 25a

CY 40a

Drayton

Beechwood Farm

Shire Lane

CY 40

CY 20

CY 14

CY 14

Parrott's Farm

Tomlin's Wood

CY 26

CY 27

CY 26

CY 23

CY 23a

CY 48r

CY 48j

Fort

Shire Lane Farm

Shire Lane

Wood

High Scrubs

Roundhill Wood

Cholesbury Bottom

Tring Grange Farm

TU 7

TU 16

TU 16

TU 14

TU 77

TU 77

TU 12

TU 12

TU 9

TU 10

TU 3

TU 3

TU 5

TU 5

A

A

B

A

B

A

A/B

A/B

N

0   1km

0   1mile

31

across a field to pass just left of a clump of bushes and reach a gap in the far hedge. Here bear slightly left across the next field to a stile just right of the far corner of the field into Parrott´s Lane at Buckland Common, again named after a village four miles to the northwest in the Vale of Aylesbury, in whose parish it was formerly located. Cross this road and take a narrow enclosed path between gateways straight on to a stile into a field. Now bear half right following a right-hand fence to a stile in the next hedge then bear slightly left across another field to a gate and stile. Here go straight on, passing through a gate and later joining a left-hand hedge to reach a gate and stile into Cholesbury Lane. Turn left onto this road and follow it back to your starting point.

WALK 6   Chartridge

Length of Walk: 4.7 miles / 7.5 Km
Starting Point: Chartridge village hall.
Grid Ref: SP930038
Maps: OS Landranger Sheet 165
            OS Explorer Sheet 2 (or old Pathfinder Sheet 1118
            (SP80/90))
            Chiltern Society FP Map No.8
How to get there / Parking: Chartridge, 2.3 miles northwest
    of the centre of Chesham, can be reached from the town
    centre by taking the road signposted to Chartridge. 300
    yards beyond the 'Bell', by the village hall, turn left into
    Cogdells Lane where there is a parking bay on the right
    or you can park at the roadside, but do **not** park opposite
    the parking bay as this can prevent cars leaving.
Notes: As the result of a legal dispute, at the time of writing,
    overgrowth blocking path C14 cannot currently be
    cleared. Should this path still be blocked, it can be
    bypassed by using the village street.

Chartridge, like its neighbours Asheridge and Bellingdon which
are visited or skirted in the course of the walk, is a long ridgetop
settlement with deep dry Chiltern bottoms on either side which
meet at Chesham to form the Chess valley. Until 1899, all three
villages, indeed, formed part of Chesham parish, which was then
the largest in Buckinghamshire, but following the parish
becoming an urban district in 1894, the rural areas soon sought
separate parish status and these three villages became part of the
new civil parish of Chartridge. Despite their former lack of
independent status and not having their own churches, all three
villages have names of Saxon origin, are recorded as long ago as
1200AD and can boast attractive farms and cottages dating back
to the sixteenth or seventeenth centuries.

    The walk, which is hilly in nature, explores the quiet and
picturesque Chiltern ridge and bottom country between the three
villages with its mixture of pasture and arable, small beechwoods
and ancient green lanes where the scene changes rapidly and fine
views abound.

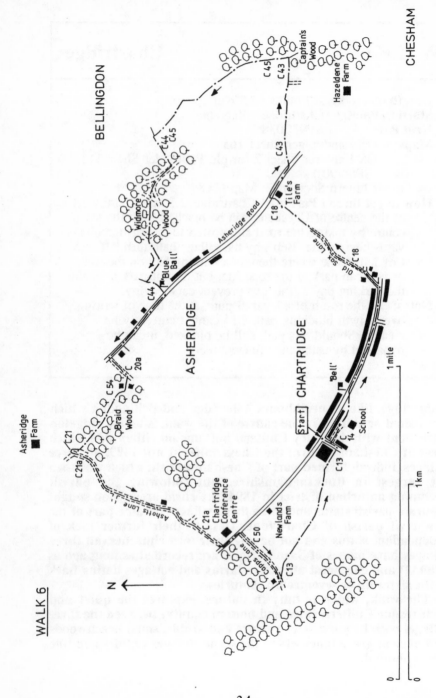

WALK 6

N ←

CHESHAM

BELLINGDON

Captains Wood

C 45
C 43

Hazeldene Farm

C 44   C 45

Widmore

Wood

Wood

"Blue Ball"

C 44

Asheridge Road

Tile's Farm

C 18

C 18

Old Sox Lane

P 10

ASHERIDGE

Asheridge Farm

C 54

C 20a

Braid Wood

C 21

C 21a

Ashotts Lane

C 21a

Chartridge Conference Centre

CHARTRIDGE

Start

"Bell"

School

C 14

C 13

Newlands Farm

C 50

Capps Lane

C 13

1 mile

1 km

0   1 km
0   1 mile

34

Starting from Chartridge village hall, take Cogdells Lane (bridleway C53). After 70 yards turn left onto path C14 along the drive to Chartridge School then take the fenced path left of the school gates to a stile into a field by a farm. (NB If still overgrown, retrace your steps to the village hall and take the Chesham road). Now bear slightly left across the field to a stile leading to the Chesham road opposite the 'Bell'. Turn right onto this road and follow it for a third of a mile, ignoring Westdean Lane to your right. Just past a telephone box, turn left into Old Sax Lane (bridleway C18), following a narrow macadam road at first. Where the macadam road turns right, leave it and take a shady green lane straight on downhill, later with views towards Chesham to your right. At the bottom of the hill, where the right-hand hedge ends, follow the left-hand hedge straight on, climbing steeply. At the top corner of the field, where this hedge peters out, follow a right-hand hedge straight on uphill to reach gates and a gap onto Asheridge Road by The Old Forge Barn at Asheridge.

Turn right onto this road and follow it for 200 yards, passing Tile's Farm to your right, then with views to your right towards the outskirts of Chesham. By a 'steep hill' sign, turn left over a stile by gates onto path C43, keeping right of a hedge and following it downhill to the bottom corner of the field. Here bear half left and cross a wooden rail then turn right and follow a right-hand hedge downhill and up again to reach the edge of Captain's Wood. Now go through a fence gap and turn left onto fenced path C45 along the outside edge of the wood. At the far end of the wood the enclosing fence ends and you continue to follow a right-hand hedge along the ridgeside for a further third of a mile.

Where the right-hand hedge bears left and then right (and path C44 to your right leads in 200 yards to Bellingdon), turn left onto path C44 following the hedge at first, then continuing downhill to enter a narrow section of Widmore Wood in the valley bottom. Just inside the wood turn right onto a track, then where the woodland widens out, go left at a fork, then immediately fork right onto a waymarked path climbing diagonally through the wood, ignoring a crossing track. At the far corner of the wood disregard another crossing track and go straight on through the right-hand of two gaps into a field, then turn left and follow a left-hand hedge around two sides of the field ignoring a stile in the hedge. On reaching the second field corner, go straight on through a hedge gap and turn left (still on path C44) following the left-hand hedge to a gate and rails. Walk round these and continue along a hedged path skirting the 'Blue Ball' car park to reach a road at Asheridge.

Turn right onto this road and follow it for a quarter mile, then, just past Braid Wood Cottage, turn left onto hedged bridleway C20a. On entering Braid Wood, turn right onto path C54, passing right of a gate between two wooden buildings and taking a paved path beside the right-hand buildings. At the far end of the buildings bear half right onto a waymarked path following the top edge of the wood for a quarter mile. Having passed through an old shallow chalkpit, turn right onto a crossing path to emerge through a fence gap at a corner of the wood. Here turn left onto path C21 then immediately left again onto fenced bridleway C21a, known as Ashotts Lane, passing through an outcrop of the wood then following a left-hand hedge downhill and up again through two fields ignoring a branching track to your right in the valley bottom. On nearing a cottage, the track widens and becomes fenced before becoming enclosed between hedges and continuing for a quarter mile to a road on the edge of Chartridge.

Turn left onto this road passing Chartridge Conference Centre, formerly known as Chartridge Lodge with its neo-classical portico. Opposite the far end of the conference centre turn right into Capps Lane (bridleway C50) and follow this rough lane for 350 yards. Just past an enlarged cottage turn left over a stile by a gate onto path C13 bearing half left across the corner of a field to join its left-hand hedge. Now follow this hedge through three fields. Where the hedge ends in the third field, go straight on to the shortest of a line of trees, then bear slightly left across the next field to a stile by Chartridge cricket pavilion. Here go straight on past the pavilion and follow a left-hand hedge to reach Cogdells Lane (bridleway C53) where you turn left for your starting point.

WALK 7   Hyde Heath

Length of Walk: 4.0 miles / 6.5 Km
Starting Point: 'The Plough', Hyde Heath.
Grid Ref: SP930004
Maps: OS Landranger Sheet 165
OS Explorer Sheet 2 (or old Pathfinder Sheet 1118 (SP80/90))
Chiltern Society FP Map No.8
How to get there / Parking: Hyde Heath, 2 miles southwest of Chesham, may be reached from the town by taking the B485 towards Great Missenden for 2.5 miles, then turning left onto a road signposted to Hyde Heath and Amersham. On entering the village, go straight on past the village green and the 'Plough', then, at the far end of the green, turn left onto a road lined with logs where you can park.
Notes: Heavy nettle growth may be encountered in places in the summer months.

Hyde Heath, with its pleasant village green on a hilltop plateau separating the Chess and Misbourne valleys, is largely a modern settlement as nineteenth-century maps show only a few scattered farms and cottages and the church and post office stores date from the 1920s while the school is Victorian. Its name, however, dates from the thirteenth century when reference occurs in a document dating from 1230 to a heath in Chesham parish belonging to William de Hyda. The link with Chesham, indeed, survived till 1899 when the rural western parts of the parish became the independent parish of Chartridge, but it was not till about 1986 that Hyde Heath, which had, hitherto, been split between three parishes finally gained official recognition by being united within the parish of Little Missenden.

The walk takes you across the common and through woodland to Hyde End and the ancient manor of Great Hundridge. You then follow the crest of a ridge with superb views descending towards the edge of Chesham before returning by way of an ancient green lane and White's Wood to Hyde Heath.

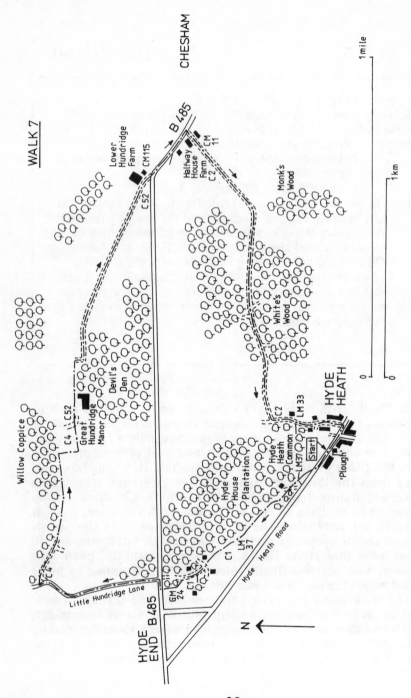

WALK 7

CHESHAM

B 485

Lower Hundridge Farm
CM 115
C 52

Halfway House
C 2
CM 11

Monk's Wood

White's Wood

Willow Coppice

C 4 C52
Great Hundridge Manor

Devil's Den

C 4
GM 24
C1

Little Hundridge Lane

HYDE END B 485

HYDE HEATH

C2
LM 33
Start
LM37
Common
Hyde Heath
'Plough'

Hyde House Plantation

C1
LM 37

Hyde Heath Road

N ←

0   1km

0   1mile

38

Starting with your back to the 'Plough` at Hyde Heath, cross the road and turn left along the edge of the village green. On reaching a footpath sign, bear half right onto path LM37 crossing the corner of the green to enter the wooded part of the common about 40 yards from the road. Now follow the waymarked path straight on through the trees, keeping straight on at a waymarked crossways to reach a cottage lawn. Go straight on across the lawn and a stone track then continue through the woods, soon with a field hedge to your left. Now follow this hedged path (later becoming C1) straight on along the edge of the wood until you emerge through a kissing-gate into a clearing by some cottages. Here take the central of three tracks straight on, soon ignoring a branching path to your left, then just past the tended hedge of a concealed cottage to your right, fork left onto waymarked path GM24 passing through more wood-land to reach the B485 at Hyde End.

Cross this fast road carefully and turn right onto its walkable far verge. At a road junction turn left into Little Hundridge Lane and take this quiet road for over a third of a mile, eventually dropping into a shallow bottom then climbing again and rounding a left-hand bend. At the far end of the bend, turn right onto path C4, soon crossing a stile to enter a fenced ride. Follow this ride straight on beside a left-hand hedge until the ride ends at a green gate. Go through this gate and follow a left-hand tree-belt then the outside edge of Willow Coppice straight on along the valley bottom until you reach the next fence. Here cross a stile and turn right following a right-hand fence steeply uphill to the top corner of the field where you turn left and follow a right-hand hedge to a stile leading to a macadam drive. Bear slightly left crossing this drive and take path C52 through a concealed walk-through stile. Now follow a sporadic right-hand hedge through a series of paddocks with views towards the outskirts of Chesham ahead and passing Great Hundridge Manor to your right. Great Hundridge Manor, first recorded as 'Hunderugg` in 1199, its name being Saxon and meaning 'hounds´ ridge`, still preserves the remains of a partially-rebuilt thirteenth-century chapel but the present house is believed to date from 1696.

On reaching a crossing hedgeline, go through a walk-through stile by a green gate, then turn right onto a grassy track beside a right-hand hedge to reach a field corner. Here turn left and follow a track along the edge of a wood called Devil´s Den. Where the wood ends and a fine view opens out ahead towards the Chess valley and Chesham, most of which is hidden by a rise, follow the grassy track straight on, descending gently for half a mile to reach

Lower Hundridge Farm. On entering the farmyard, take path CM115 straight on past the farmhouse to reach a bend in the B485.

Cross this fast road carefully, then turn left along its far verge and follow it for 300 yards ignoring a branching path to your right. Just past Halfway House Farm turn right onto bridleway CM11 following a macadam farm drive into a sunken green lane which soon becomes bridleway C2 and gently ascends the valley bottom, eventually entering White's Wood. Follow the obvious track straight on along the woodland bottom, soon passing a grass field to your right, then bearing slightly left and climbing more steeply ignoring branching tracks to left and right. On leaving the wood, continue between hedges until you emerge into a stony lane. Turn left into this lane and follow it (soon on bridleway LM33) back to Hyde Heath where your starting point is to your right.

WALK 8   Great Missenden

Length of Walk: 3.6 miles / 5.8 Km
Starting Point: Northwest corner of car park in Link Road, Great Missenden.
Grid Ref: SP894015
Maps: OS Landranger Sheet 165
OS Explorer Sheet 2 (or old Pathfinder Sheet 1118 (SP80/90))
Chiltern Society FP Map No.12
How to get there / Parking: Great Missenden, 4.7 miles northwest of Amersham, may be reached from the town by following the A413 to the twin roundabouts at its junction with the B485 and A4128. At the second roundabout, turn left onto the A4128, where, after 200 yards, there is a car park on the right.

Great Missenden, near the source of the fitful River Misbourne at Mobwell, has a long, narrow, picturesque High Street flanked by a number of old coaching inns, cottages and small shops, some dating back to the fifteenth and sixteenth centuries and is typical of a small town astride an old turnpike road. Apparently there were many more coaching inns in the past, but the arrival of the Metropolitan Railway in 1892 led to a loss of trade. Thanks to the town´s bypass, which was controversial when it was constructed because it sliced through Abbey Park and cut the church off from the town, it is possible to appreciate the High Street´s old world charm. The fourteenth-century church with its Norman font on the site of a Saxon predecessor stands in a prominent hillside location on the edge of Abbey Park. The Abbey itself, which was founded by William de Missenden in 1133 and was in the Middle Ages one of the largest in the county, has recently had to be rebuilt following a disastrous fire which gutted the late eighteenth-century building.

The walk, which is easy in nature, leads you gently up a valley bottom through Angling Spring Wood to reach the suburban hilltop village of Prestwood. You then turn north, descend through Rignall Wood to Rignall Road and climb again to the top of Coney Hill where fine views open out down the Misbourne valley towards Great Missenden and you drop down to Mobwell

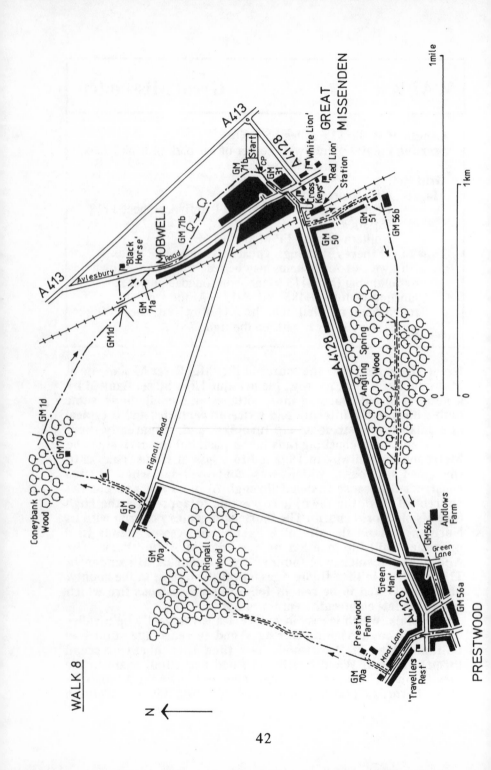

WALK 8

N ←

MOBWELL

GREAT MISSENDEN

A413

A413

A4128

A413

Aylesbury

'Black Horse'

GM 71a

GM 1d

GM 71b

GM 71b

Start

CP

GM 31

'White Lion'

'Cross Keys'

'Red Lion'

Station

GM 50

GM 51

GM 56b

Angling Spring Wood

A4128

Rignall Road

GM 1d

GM 70

GM 70

GM 70a

GM 70a

Coneybank Wood

Rignall Wood

Prestwood Farm

Moat Lane

'Travellers' Rest'

'Green Man'

A4128

GM 56a

GM 56b

Green Lane

Andlows Farm

PRESTWOOD

1 mile

1 km

0

42

and continue back to your starting point.

Starting from the rear left-hand corner of the car park in Link
Road, Great Missenden, go through a gap in the fence and turn left
onto enclosed path GM31, soon reaching the end of Walnut Close.
Follow this road to a T-junction, then turn left then right onto the
High Wycombe road passing the railway station and crossing a
bridge over the railway. At the far end of the bridge turn left into a
rough road called Trafford Road (path GM50). After 300 yards,
by the near end of a terrace of cottages, turn right onto path GM51,
passing the end of the terrace and crossing a stile into a field. Now
bear half left across the field to a gate by the corner of a garden
hedge, where you bear half right onto path GM56b and follow a
left-hand fence up the valley bottom to a gate and stile into
Angling Spring Wood. In the wood follow an obvious track straight
on up the valley bottom ignoring all crossing or branching tracks
or paths. At the far side of the wood go straight on through a
kissing-gate and take a sunken path straight on beside a right-hand
hedge. Where the hedge bears right, take an old sunken track
straight on up the bottom of the dip, eventually joining a right-
hand hedge. At a field corner continue along a narrow enclosed
path to reach the junction of Green Lane, to which the former
Labour prime minister, Clement Attlee, retired following his defeat
in 1951, and New Road at Prestwood.
   Like a number of other Chiltern villages, Prestwood was once
famous for its cherry orchards, which produced the local Prestwood
Blacks, used to make the Buckinghamshire speciality of cherry pie
before the orchards gave way to modern housing estates in the
1960s and 1970s.
   Continue along New Road, then, at its far end, take an alleyway
(path GM56a) straight on, passing an old pond to reach the
junction of Nairdwood Lane and Honor Road. Turn right into
Nairdwood Lane and follow it to its junction with the A4128 (High
Street) where the 'Travellers' Rest` is to your left. Cross the main
road and take Moat Lane straight on, soon rounding a left-hand
bend. After about 200 yards turn right onto path GM70a,
following the concrete drive to Prestwood Farm. Where the drive
turns right into the farmyard, go straight on over a stile by an
electricity pole and follow a left-hand fence to a gate and stile.
Here go straight on through a former gateway and follow a right-
hand hedge, soon joining a grassy track which merges from your
right and following it to a corner of Rignall Wood. Now fork right
off the track into the wood, keeping left at a fork and disregarding

a crossing path, then continue downhill through the wood ignoring two further crossing paths. On leaving the wood, take a fenced path beside a left-hand hedge, eventually passing some buildings and emerging onto a private drive which you follow out to Rignall Road on the outskirts of Great Missenden.

Turn right onto its near verge, then, after 100 yards, where the verge narrows, turn left crossing the road and taking path GM70 down a stony lane. Ignore a branching path to your right, then, where the lane bears right into a private garden and ends, leave it and take an enclosed path straight on uphill into Coneybank Wood. On entering the wood, bear half right and follow the obvious path uphill through it to a stile into a field at the top of Coney Hill. Cross this stile and turn right onto path GM1d with a fine view opening out ahead down the Misbourne valley towards Great Missenden with its prominent church. Where the edge of the wood bears away to the right, bear slightly right to the bottom corner of the field, where you descend some steps to cross a stile. Now go straight on across the next field to cross another stile, then continue across a further field to a gate and stile leading to a railway arch. Pass under the railway then fork right onto path GM71a crossing a field diagonally to a stile in the far corner onto Aylesbury Road at Mobwell.

Turn right along the road. After 150 yards, by the far end of a row of terraced cottages, turn left crossing the road and a stile by a gate into a field and take path GM71b bearing half right and joining a left-hand hedge. At the far end of the field cross a stile between gates and continue along a fenced path to reach a fence gap leading into the car park.

WALK 9   Hampden Row

Length of Walk: (A) 4.7 miles / 7.5 Km
                    (B) 4.5 miles / 7.3 Km
Starting Point: Crossroads by the 'Hampden Arms',
                    Hampden Row.
Grid Ref: SP845015
Maps: OS Landranger Sheet 165
              OS Explorer Sheet 2 (or old Pathfinder Sheet 1118
              (SP80/90))
              Chiltern Society FP Maps Nos. 3 & 12
How to get there / Parking: Hampden Row, 5.4 miles north-
      west of High Wycombe, may be reached from the town by
      taking the A4128 northwards for two miles and leaving it
      at a roundabout where it turns right. Now go straight on
      up the Hughenden Valley for a further three-quarters of a
      mile. By the 'Harrow' turn right and, after half a mile, turn
      left following signs to Bryant's Bottom. Take this road
      through Bryant's Bottom for 2.3 miles to a crossroads,
      then turn right towards Hampden and Great Missenden
      and at a T-junction, turn right again. At a road junction
      by the 'Hampden Arms', turn right and seek a suitable
      parking place along this quiet road.

Hampden Row, the village attached to the Great Hampden
Estate, is typical of many such estate villages in being some
distance from its church and manor house on the edge of the
parish common. Its name is apt as it consists of a pub and row of
cottages along one side of a road with the common on the other
with a particularly attractive cricket field set out by the last Earl
of Buckinghamshire in 1950. Hampden Row, one-time home of
the late Poet Laureate, John Masefield, derives its name from the
Hampden family (later the Earls of Buckinghamshire) whose
most famous member was John Hampden (1594 - 1643), the
leading Parliamentarian and soldier and cousin of Oliver
Cromwell. His refusal to pay Ship Money in 1635 led to a writ
being served upon him at Hampden House and this was one of
the significant events leading to the Civil War. This battlemented
fourteenth-century house, considerably altered both by John
Hampden and again in the eighteenth century and with ceilings

45

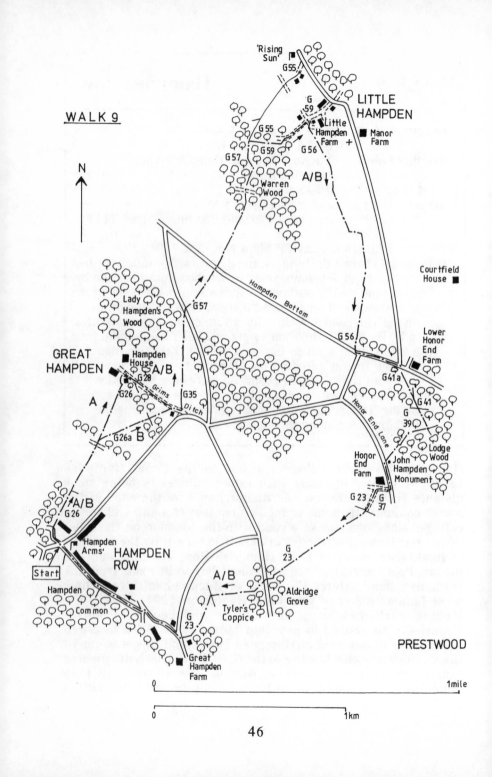

WALK 9

N

'Rising Sun'
G55
LITTLE HAMPDEN
G 59
G 55
Little Hampden Farm +
Manor Farm
G 57
G 59
G 56
A/B↓
Warren Wood

Courtfield House ■

Hampden Bottom

G 57

Lady Hampden's Wood

G 56
Lower Honor End Farm

GREAT HAMPDEN ■
Hampden House
A/B
G 28
G26
A
Grims
Ditch
G35
G 41a
G 41
G 39
Lodge Wood
G 26a B

Honor End Lane

Honor End Farm
John Hampden Monument

A/B
G 26

'Hampden Arms'
HAMPDEN ROW

Start

G 23
G 37

Hampden Common

A/B
G 23

Aldridge Grove

G 23
Tyler's Coppice

Great Hampden Farm

PRESTWOOD

0   1mile

0   1km

46

and fireplaces by Adam, is passed in the course of the walk, as is Great Hampden´s thirteenth-century church, where John Hampden was buried in an unmarked grave after being mortally wounded at Chalgrove Field. The church contains various monuments to the Hampden family including one erected to John Hampden in the eighteenth century.

Both walks, which have fine views in places, tour the Hampden country, first leading you past Great Hampden Church and Hampden House before crossing Hampden Bottom to reach the edge of Little Hampden, which has often been described as the ´most remote village in the Buckinghamshire Chilterns`. You then return by a more easterly route recrossing Hampden Bottom and passing the John Hampden Monument before returning to Hampden Row.

Both walks start from the crossroads by the ´Hampden Arms` at Hampden Row and take an unsignposted road westwards across the common rounding a right-hand bend. At a left-hand bend leave the road and take enclosed path G26 straight on, soon passing through gates and continuing past a copse to enter a field. Here take what is normally a crop-break straight on, aiming for the left-hand end of a clump of tall oaks, where you cross a farm road and continue between the oaks and a coniferous plantation to gates into a parkland field where Great Hampden Church, with its short high nave and disproportionately small tower, comes into view ahead. Now, for a closer look at the church and Hampden House, **Walk A** takes path G26 straight on, following a left-hand fence through a series of kissing-gates to the church, then turns right down the Hampden House drive (bridleway G28) to rejoin Walk B. **Walk B** bears half right onto path G26a crossing the large parkland field diagonally, passing just left of a pair of massive lime trees to reach a kissing-gate left of a brick-&-flint lodge. Go through this and a second kissing-gate and turn right onto the Hampden House drive (bridleway G28) passing through the lodge gate.

Both walks now turn left over a stile by a gate onto path G35 bearing slightly left across a field, aiming well left of a clump of tall conifers to reach a stile with a fine view of Hampden House to your left. Now go straight on downhill to cross a stile by gates onto a road by the bottom right-hand corner of Lady Hampden´s Wood. Bear half left across this road passing through a hedge gap and taking path G57 beside a right-hand hedge downhill to the road along Hampden Bottom. Cross this fast road carefully and take path G57 straight on through a hedge gap, following a left-hand

47

hedge uphill to a hedge gap into Warren Wood. Take an obvious waymarked path uphill through the wood, ignoring a crossing track and then levelling out. Near the far side of the wood at a way-marked path junction, turn right onto path G59 along the inside edge of the wood at first, then continuing along a green lane to a track junction by Warren Cottage on the edge of Little Hampden with its small thirteenth-century church with thirteenth- and fifteenth-century murals rediscovered in 1907 and an unusual pointed doorway made from naturally curved oak trunks, as well as two interesting farms dating from at least the seventeenth century.

Here turn right onto path G56 following a grassy track beside a left-hand hedge past the back of Little Hampden Farm. Where the main track turns left towards a green barn, leave it and take a hedged path straight on. Eventually the right-hand hedge ends and the left-hand hedge becomes lower to reveal a fine view across Hampden Bottom towards Courtfield House and the edge of Prestwood in trees on the skyline. Now continue beside the left-hand hedge winding gently downhill to the bottom corner of the field. Here turn left through a hedge gap then right and follow the other side of the hedge beneath a powerline for a further 250 yards to the corner of a plantation. Now continue between a hedge and the plantation to reach the road in Hampden Bottom.

Turn left onto this road, ignoring a turning to your right and continuing to Little Hampden Turn. Here turn right over a stile onto path G41a and follow it through a wood. Near the far side of the wood join path G41 merging from your left and follow it over a stile into a narrow field known as The Glade, created to provide a vista from Hampden House, which can be seen in the distance to your right. To your left are a pair of octagonal, eighteenth-century lodges called The Pepperboxes. Follow a right-hand fence straight on across this field, then cross another stile and take a fenced path along the edge of Lodge Wood. Where the right-hand field gives way to woodland, turn right onto crossing path G39 and follow it along the inside edge of the wood to cross a stile at a corner of the wood. Now follow a right-hand fence uphill crossing two stiles and reaching Honor End Lane by the John Hampden Monument.

Turn left onto this road and follow it uphill past the monument and Honor End Farm. By the far end of the farm buildings, turn right through gates onto path G37 passing through a further gate into a concrete yard. Here turn left through a former gateway onto path G23 and take a grassy track across a field to a gate at the corner of a fence. Do NOT go through this gate, but bear slightly right and follow a left-hand fence, then a hedge straight on through two fields, later with a wood called Aldridge Grove to your left. On nearing the far end of the second field, where you start to descend into a shallow bottom, the path turns left into the wood and then bears right and follows its inside edge downhill to Hampden Road.

Cross this road and go through a fence gap opposite, then take a winding waymarked path uphill through Tyler´s Coppice, soon with a field to your right. On emerging at a corner of the wood, keep right of a hedge and follow it to its far end. Here bear half left, ignoring a crossing path, passing left of a large oak tree and heading for a twin-poled electricity pylon at the corner of a mature plantation, where you bear slightly right and follow a left-hand hedge to a corner of the field. Now bear slightly right again through a hedge gap into a copse of poplars and follow a left-hand hedge through the copse to a road junction. Here bear half right onto a road passing a wooden shed and follow it downhill to another junction, where you bear slightly left, joining the priority road and follow it for a third of a mile along the edge of Hampden Common to your starting point.

WALK 10   Great Kimble

Length of Walk: 4.1 miles / 6.6 Km
Starting Point: Northeastern end of layby at Great Kimble.
Grid Ref: SP825059
Maps: OS Landranger Sheet 165
OS Explorer Sheet 2 (or old Pathfinder Sheet 1118 (SP80/90))
Chiltern Society FP Map No.3
How to get there / Parking: Great Kimble, 2 miles northeast of Princes Risborough, may be reached from the town by taking the A4010 towards Aylesbury. At the ´Black Horse` roundabout at Askett, go straight on over a rise, then at a slight left-hand bend turn right into an unmarked layby with a white thatched cottage.

Great Kimble, at the foot of the Chiltern escarpment, appears from the A4010 to be little more than a church and a pub, but the village is hidden down a lane. Despite being small, Great Kimble has played a major role in history as the ancient British king Cunobelinus, also known as Cymbeline, after whom the village is named, had a fortress on a nearby hill called Cymbeline´s Mount before the Roman invasion in 43AD and ancient British and Roman remains were found in a tumulus near the church in 1887. In 1635 the heavily-restored thirteenth-century church was the scene of John Hampden´s refusal to pay Ship Money, of which he disputed the legality and this was the first in a series of events leading to the Civil War. In recent years the village´s proximity to Chequers has led to the ´Bernard Arms` being frequented by leading politicians including a famous visit by Prime Minister John Major and Russian President Boris Yeltsin.

The walk leads you from Great Kimble along the foot of the escarpment to the villages of Askett, Monks Risborough and Whiteleaf with their picturesque cottages before climbing through woods to Longdown Hill. You then return by way of the slopes of Pulpit Hill with superb views across the Vale of Aylesbury.

Starting from the northeastern end of the layby at Great Kimble, cross the A4010 and take path K1 opposite, part of the North Bucks Way, through a kissing-gate into a field. Bear slightly left across this field heading for a large house called Old Grange to cross a stile by an electricity pole. Now take path K1b bearing slightly right across the next field to a stile in front of a small thatched summerhouse. Here cross a drive and pass right of the summerhouse to cross a further stile, then bear slightly right across a field to a double-stile in the far corner. Cross both parts of this stile and leaving the North Bucks Way, turn left onto path K1c following a left-hand fence. At the far end of the field cross a stile and keep straight on to the corner of a hedge ahead where you go through a hedge gap and take path R29 straight on beside a left-hand hedge through three fields to a stile by the corner of a brick-and-flint garage block by the ´Three Crowns` at Askett.

Cross this stile to emerge onto a road then turn right and almost immediately left into Askett Lane. Follow this narrow road past a number of picturesque timbered cottages. At its far end, turn left onto enclosed path R33 leading to a gate and stile. Here turn right onto path R34 following a right-hand wall, later a hedge, through a belt of trees to a stile. Now follow the right-hand hedge straight on with views to your left of Whiteleaf Hill, crossing two more stiles and looking out for a concealed stile in the right-hand hedge. Here take path R35a bearing half left across the field to cross a footbridge and stile in its far corner, then continue along a winding fenced path to Mill Lane at Monks Risborough. Although Monks Risborough is now joined to Princes Risborough by the latter´s modern housing estates, the old village, once a separate parish, with its sixteenth-century square white-stone dovecote, its fine array of sixteenth- and seventeenth-century cottages and its fine fourteenth-century church which appears to have been rebuilt on the site of an earlier building as its font is Norman, its tower is older than the rest of the church and its dedication to the Saxon St. Dunstan suggests pre-conquest origin, preserves its quiet rural atmosphere.

Cross Mill Lane and take a path straight on into the churchyard. By the church tower follow the path bearing left. At a fork by the church door turn right leaving the churchyard by a gate and continuing along Burton Lane. Where its surface becomes macadamed, ignore a turning to your left and continue to the service road beside the A4010. Turn left onto its footway, soon crossing the end of Mill Lane. At a pelican crossing, cross the A4010 and take fenced path R26 through a kissing-gate left of a school. Follow it to a kissing-gate into a field, then bear half left along a worn path across the field to a corner. Here go through a kissing-gate and continue between fences to join the verge of The Holloway at Whiteleaf. Best known for the large ancient cross carved into the chalk hillside above the village, Whiteleaf can also boast some fine sixteenth- and seventeenth-century cottages.

Bear right onto this verge climbing to a T-junction then turn left onto the Upper Icknield Way. After 70 yards turn right into Thorns Lane (bridleway R18) and go uphill ignoring branching drives to your right and a path to your left. On entering Giles Wood, disregard a branching path to your right and continue uphill to the top of the rise. At a track junction take bridleway R18a straight on along a track past a thatched cottage to your left. By a double garage the track narrows and drops steeply (beware : slippery chalk surface!), then follows the inside edge of the wood bearing left and then right and climbing over a further rise. At the bottom of the next dip, just past a right-hand gate at a left-hand bend, fork right onto path R15 up some steps then turning left and following a left-hand fence to the Ridgeway Path. Cross this and take waymarked path R15a bearing slightly right through an area of storm-ravaged woodland, later keeping left at a fork and eventually dropping steeply to a staggered junction of tracks. Here turn left then immediately right and at a three-way junction, keep left passing left of a noticeboard and taking path R24a along the right-hand side of a valley bottom. Where this track forks, go right, taking a sunken way steeply uphill into Ninn Wood. About halfway up the hill turn left by a waymarking post onto a winding path through a plantation. At the edge of mature woodland, go left at a T-junction and take a waymarked track to the far side of the wood. Here cross a stile and turn left onto bridleway R23 ignoring a branching path to your right and taking the fenced bridleway along the edge of the wood for over a quarter mile to the road at Longdown Hill.

Cross this road and take bridleway K41 straight on into Pulpit Wood passing a car park to your left. By a gate ignore a crossing path and go straight on, dropping gently and soon passing a steep-sided coombe to your left. By another coombe to your left, just before a left-hand stile, fork right onto terraced path K47 climbing at first then following the contours of the hill through the wood to a kissing-gate where fine views open out to your left across the Vale of Aylesbury and Oxfordshire Plain. Here take a worn path straight on through scrubby downland rich in orchids and other rare chalkland plants to the Ridgeway Path, where you take a less obvious path straight on, heading for a stile on the next rise, before crossing which you cross a concealed stile in the dip. Now keep straight on to a further stile left of a gate leading into bridleway K40, part of the North Bucks Way. Turn left onto this ancient lane and follow it gently downhill to your starting point.

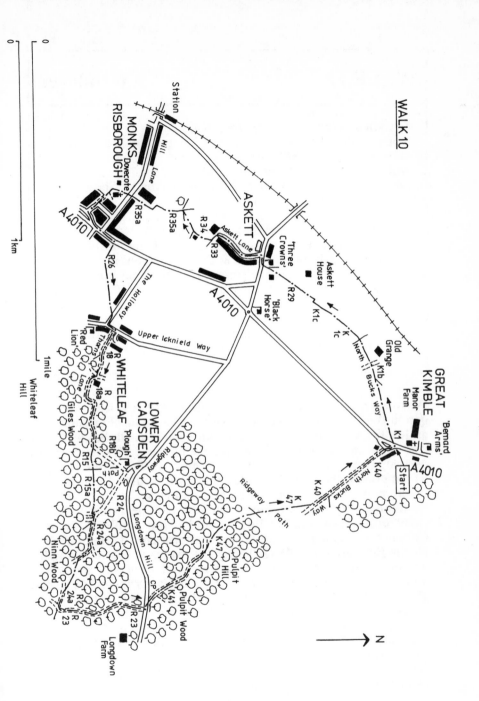

WALK 10

N →

53

WALK 11   Wendover

Length of Walk: 5.4 miles / 8.8 Km
Starting Point: ´Rose & Crown`, Tring Road, Wendover.
Grid Ref: SP874083
Maps: OS Landranger Sheet 165
          OS Explorer Sheet 2 (or old Pathfinder Sheets 1094
          (SP81/91) & 1118 (SP80/90))
          Chiltern Society FP Map No.18
How to get there / Parking: From the clocktower roundabout
   in Wendover take the B4009 towards Tring for 0.4 miles,
   looking out for the ´Rose & Crown` on your right, where
   you turn right into the continuation of Tring Road. Now,
   after 100 yards park in a small car park on your right or
   find a suitable on-street parking space. Do **not** use the pub
   car park without the landlord´s permission.
Notes: Heavy nettle growth may be encountered, particularly
   on path A11, in the summer months.

Wendover, an ancient borough on the Upper Icknield Way at a gap in the Chiltern escarpment, would seem to be of considerable antiquity. Not only is it located on an ancient road, but also Iron Age pottery was found here and its name is of Celtic origin deriving from ´Gwyn-dwfr` meaning ´holy `or ´fair water`. Despite its smallness, from 1625 to 1832 the town returned two MPs to Parliament including such famous names as John Hampden, Edmund Burke, Richard Steele (founder of ´The Tatler`) and the early nineteenth-century foreign and prime minister, George Canning, but along with other ´rotten boroughs` it was abolished by the Reform Act in 1832. Today the centre of the town retains its old world charm thanks to a wealth of Georgian shops and houses as well as a number of older cottages including a row given to Henry VIII as part of Catherine of Aragon´s dowry.

The walk soon leads you out of the town into the extensive Wendover Woods climbing to a superb viewpoint at Aston Hill. You then descend with further fine views to reach the leafy Wendover Arm canal towpath on the edge of Green Park, Aston Clinton, before following the canal to Halton village, whence you return across open fields into Wendover.

Starting with your back to the ´Rose & Crown`, turn left along Tring Road. At a fork where Beechwood Lane and Warneford Avenue branch to the right, take path W24 straight on through a fence gap right of a small brick building. Now follow a right-hand fence through grassland at first, then straight on into scrub. Here keep straight on for 400 yards, ignoring all lesser branching paths and a crossing macadam path, then continue with a hedge to your right until your way ahead is blocked and you turn right over a footbridge into an area of parkland. Now turn left and follow a left-hand hedge to a corner of the park where you go straight on through a hedge gap and turn left onto a crossing concrete path. Take this to a fence gap onto a private road. Do **NOT** join this road but turn right, passing right of the gates of a fenced compound and following a left-hand fence. On reaching a hedge, turn left onto a fenced path to cross another private road. Now take a macadam path (still W24) straight on beside a line of sycamore trees then continuing between buildings and descending to cross a macadam track at the edge of woodland. Here take macadam path H5 straight on through the woods to a bend in a private road. Do **NOT** join this road but bear slightly right to enter Halton Wood, where you join a track along its edge by a line of ancient beech trees.

Now disregard a branching horse-track and a crossing track and take a terraced hillside track (still path H5) straight on for over a third of a mile, ignoring a steep crossing path and eventually reaching a crossing sunken way. Turn left onto this then fork immediately right onto a narrow terraced path, soon climbing steeply and ignoring a crossing path (where Walk 12 is a quarter mile to your right). Now continue, soon between flint walls, to reach a major crossing track. Cross this and continue up a flight of steps, then take path A26 straight on through woodland, climbing gently to a Forestry Commission road. Having crossed this, climb a flight of steps and continue uphill, keeping right at a fork then passing under an overhanging beech tree and bearing right to reach a stone track. Turn left onto this then, after 50 yards, turn right over a stile into a field. Bear half left crossing this field diagonally and passing left of an old trig point to cross a stile into scrub in the far corner of the field. Go straight on through this to a road, onto which you turn left towards Aston Hill car park with its fine view over Wilstone Reservoir and the Vale of Aylesbury towards Mentmore Towers on its prominent ridge which was built for Baron Mayer de Rothschild by Sir Joseph Paxton, designer of the Crystal Palace, in 1852.

Just before the car park turn right onto path A13, passing an old gate and taking a stone track into woodland. After 150 yards turn left onto path A12, immediately forking left again and following a left-hand sunken way through scrubby woodland for a third of a mile disregarding all branching paths. Eventually you descend into the sunken way and ignore a crossing path before emerging by a clubhouse onto a golf course. Here follow a white fence, then a line of white posts straight on to the edge of a belt of scrub. Follow this along the edge of the course until you pass a gate to your left. Here bear slightly right to pass right of a shed and a tee and enter a fenced path with fine views ahead of Ivinghoe Beacon and Pitstone Hill, which you follow to the junction of the B489 and B4009.

Cross the B4009 here and turn left onto its footway. At the next junction turn right over a stile onto path A11 downhill through woodland, bearing right at a fork into a sunken way. Eventually the sunken way gives way to open woodland and you reach a kissing-gate onto the towpath of the Wendover Arm of the Grand Union Canal opened in 1796. Turn left onto this towpath (path A41, later H18) and follow it for a mile with Green Park to your right at first, briefly permitting a view towards Aylesbury and the distinctive County Hall (otherwise known as 'Pooley's Castle`). You then pass under Harelane Bridge and continue with views to your right towards Halton Airfield and a possible glimpse in trees some way to your left of Halton House, built in 1884 in the French style for Baron Alfred de Rothschild, later passing under an ornamental bridge bearing the Rothschild crest to reach Halton village street.

Turn left onto this road passing the church built in 1813 in the trees to your left and continuing to a road junction. Here turn right, then by the junction with Clayfield Road, turn left onto path H6 bearing slightly right across a playing field to cross a stile midway along an avenue of trees on its right-hand boundary. Now bear half left across a field heading for a clump of small trees. By the corner of an old field boundary, bear slightly right to cross a stile. Here go straight on across a narrow field to pass through a concealed hedge gap left of a small tree and cross a footbridge into a field. Now take path W1 bearing slightly right across the field to a stile into a belt of scrub, then continue through this, soon climbing several steps to cross a former railway and a stile. Here bear half right across the next field, crossing a rise and continuing to the corner of a playing field fence. Now bear half left following the fence and a sporadic hedge for 350 yards to a stile onto a concrete drive on the edge of Wendover. Go straight on up this drive to Manor Crescent, then turn left and take this road gradually bearing right to reach a T-junction with Manor Road. Here turn left and follow it uphill to the B4009 where you turn left again for your starting point.

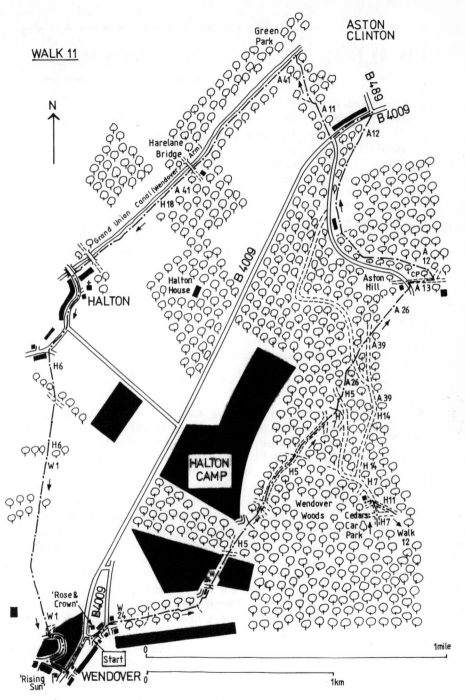

WALK 11

N

ASTON
CLINTON

Green
Park

A41

A 11

B 489

B 4009

A12

Harelane
Bridge

Grand Union Canal (Wendover Arm)

A 41

H 18

A 12

CP

B 4009

HALTON

Halton
House

Aston
Hill

A 13

A 26

H6

A39

A 26

H5

A 39

H
7

H14

H6

W1

HALTON
CAMP

H5

H 14

H7

H11

Wendover
Woods

Cedars
Car
Park

H7

Walk
12

H5

'Rose &
Crown'

B 4009

W
24

W1

Start

'Rising
Sun'

WENDOVER

0   1mile

0   1km

57

WALK 12   Wendover Woods

Length of Walk: 5.3 miles / 8.6 Km
Starting Point: Entrance to toilets at central car parking area in Wendover Woods.
Grid Ref: SP889090
Maps: OS Landranger Sheet 165
OS Explorer Sheet 2 (or old Pathfinder Sheet 1118 (SP80/90))
Chiltern Society FP Maps Nos. 3 & 8
How to get there / Parking: Wendover Woods, 1.5 miles northeast of Wendover, may be reached from the town by taking the A4011 towards Tring for 2 miles through Halton, then turning right onto the St. Leonards, Cholesbury and Chesham road. After 300 yards, after rounding a right-hand bend, turn right onto a one-way Forestry Commission road and follow it for just over a mile to the central car parking area with several small car parks.
Notes: Nettle and bramble growth may be encountered in places particularly in the summer months.

Wendover Woods are an extensive area of Forestry Commission woodland to the northeast of Wendover on the highest ridge in the Chilterns. Today these woods are popular due to the recreational facilities provided by the Commission and their excellent network of public and permissive paths. In recognition of its efforts in setting this up, the Commission received a Countryside Award in 1970. In the past, however, the Chiltern woods provided a hide-out for outlaws such as Sir Adam de Gurdon who was dispossessed of his estates for siding with de Montfort in the Barons' War. Tracked down in Wendover Woods by the future King Edward I in 1266, Sir Adam was defeated by Edward in single combat but is said to have won Edward's admiration for his valour, as a result of which the two became friends.

This walk explores the southeastern part of the woods including a section of ridgeside track with spectacular views across the Wendover gap. It also leads you through the remote area of countryside around Chivery to the east where further woodland is interspersed with quiet pockets of farmland.

Starting with your back to the entrances to the wooden toilet building in the central parking area of Wendover Woods, turn left to reach the stone cairn marking the Countryside Award, then bear half right, passing right of a seat and a large cedar tree, and take path H11 straight on between bollards onto a stone track, soon joining the continuation of the Forestry Commission road. Ignore a crossing path then, at a right-hand bend, turn left onto the second of two branching paths (A23) following a firebreak with a power-line for 75 yards until a waymark directs you to branch right into scrubby woodland. Now take the obvious path straight on for some 300 yards to a T-junction with path A22, where you bear half right onto it and follow it to a stile into a field. Go straight on across this field to a kissing-gate in the far hedge left of a house.

Go through this and turn left onto a road descending to pass Southpark House where you ignore a branching bridleway to your right and then climbing again. Just before a left-hand bend turn right over a rail-stile onto path A16 bearing slightly left across a field to a stile in the far hedge by a corner of Bittam´s Wood. Now follow the outside edge of the wood straight on to a stile into it. Turn left over this stile and take the waymarked path straight on through the wood, ignoring a branching path to your right and reaching a crossing firebreak. Continue across this and downhill through the wood to a waymarked crossways. Here turn right onto path A14. On reaching a crossing firebreak, go straight on descending gently for 200 yards. Where the path begins to drop more steeply, turn right over a stile then left following the left-hand fence downhill along the outside edge of the wood, ignoring a rail-stile in the fence in the valley bottom then continuing uphill to a gate and rail-stile into Black Wood. Turn left over this stile, in a few yards reaching a hairpin bend in a narrow road known as The Crong.

Turn left down this road, ignoring a branching path to your right. At the entrance to Dancers End Pumping Station, turn right onto path B29 up the drive to this fine example of Victorian civic architecture. Go straight on through an ornate red-brick gateway into a yard. By a line of garages, turn left, soon going through a gate and taking a fenced path straight on into Northill Wood. Having crossed a stile, continue beside the left-hand fence past a left-hand field to a waymarked crossways. Here take bridleway DB28 straight on to join a left-hand hedge, then ignore a branching path into the left-hand field and continue along the bottom inside edge of Pavis Wood. On nearing a road at Paines End, near a concealed County Council noticeboard to your right, turn sharp right onto path DB27 uphill through the wood to enter a sunken way. Near the top of the hill ignore a branching path to your left, then leave the sunken way and skirt a left-hand plantation and deep pit to cross the Ridgeway Path. On leaving the wood, take path B25 bearing slightly left across the field to cross a distant stile in front of a wooden electricity pylon. Now turn right onto bridleway CY7 and follow this macadam private road to and through Leylands Farm to a road. Turn right onto this then almost immediately left over a concealed stile onto path CY49 following a right-hand hedge downhill to a stile into scrubland. Bear half left onto an obvious winding path through the scrubland. On entering a field, follow a left-hand fence straight on soon with a tree-belt to your right. At the end of the tree-belt take a macadam drive straight on to a road at Lanes End on the edge of the remote village of St. Leonards.

Turn right onto this road for a quarter mile to a row of cottages on your left at Chivery. Just past a cottage called ´The Old Plough`, formerly the hamlet pub, turn left through gates by a wooden shed onto path A19 going straight on through the garden to gates into a field. Bear slightly left across this field to cross a stile in its far left-hand corner, then take path W42e bearing half left across the next field to the corner of a hedge. Here turn right onto path W42, soon crossing a stile by a gate and following the right-hand hedge to Milesfield Farm. Now cross the farm drive and take a concrete track straight on between barns into a field, where you follow a right-hand fence and sporadic hedge to cross a stile into Hale Wood. Here follow a path beneath a powerline, soon crossing the Ridgeway Path and dropping steeply to leave the wood by a fence gap and continue beneath the powerline across the valley with fine views across The Hale towards Bacombe Hill. On reaching the edge of Halton Wood, bear slightly left and follow it towards The Hale.

Where a tree-belt commences to your left, turn right over a stile down a flight of steps into a sunken bridleway then climb the steep bank opposite. At the top of the bank turn right onto path H21 crossing a stile by a gate into Halton Wood. Now follow a sunken way gently uphill, gradually bearing left to reach a grassy clearing. Here turn left and take a wide track ignoring a crossing horse track then later bearing right to reach a fork. Now take the right-hand option straight on, joining path H7 merging from your right and following a wide stone terraced track for half a mile ignoring all branching paths. On reaching a major fork, take the right-hand option straight on, climbing gently, soon with wide views to your left towards Cock´s Hill, Bacombe Hill and Boddington Hill. Eventually the track bears right and climbs more steeply, soon reaching a gate onto the Forestry Commission road near your starting point.

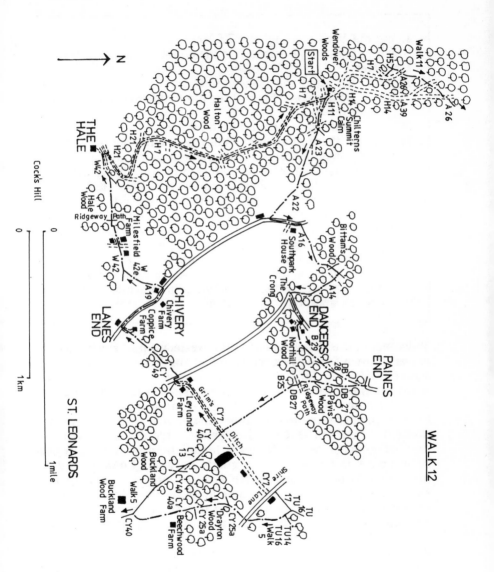

WALK 12

N →

Cock's Hill

ST. LEONARDS

0 — 1km

0 — 1mile

61

Length of Walk: 4.7 miles / 7.5 Km
Starting Point: Wilstone War Memorial.
Grid Ref: SP905140
Maps: OS Landranger Sheet 165
OS Explorer Sheet 2 (or old Pathfinder Sheet 1094 (SP81/91))
Chiltern Society FP Map No.18
How to get there / Parking: Wilstone, 2 miles northwest of Tring, may be reached from the roundabout at the western end of the Tring Bypass by taking the A41 towards Aylesbury for 1.2 miles to a mini-roundabout at Aston Clinton. Here turn right onto the B489 towards Dunstable and follow it for 1.7 miles, then some 350 yards beyond a sharp double bend, turn left for Wilstone. In the village look out for a small green to your right with the war memorial then find a suitable parking place.
Notes: If and when the planned A41 Aston Clinton Bypass is built, it will cross the walk route near Drayton Beauchamp Church and north of Buckland.

Wilstone, in the Tring salient at the western tip of Hertfordshire, is best known for its reservoir, one of the Tring reservoirs constructed between 1802 and 1839 to provide water to the highest point on the Grand Junction Canal (since 1929 known as the Grand Union Canal) after the leaky Wendover Arm canal built for this purpose had proved inadequate. Just as the main canal, (built by the third Duke of Bridgewater from nearby Ashridge and his engineer friend, James Brindley, between 1793 and 1806 to improve the transport of goods between London and the industrial Midlands and North and serving this purpose until superceded by the railways and modern road transport), has now been adapted for recreational use, the reservoirs have now become nature reserves frequented by many rare species of waterfowl and are also popular with anglers. The village, however, which has only had its own church since 1860, also gained notoriety in 1751 when a suspected witch called Ruth Osborn was hounded by the local populace and murdered by a chimneysweep called Colley who allegedly held her head under water in a local pond. While some say that these events took place in nearby Long Marston, what is definitely known, is that Colley was tried and hanged in the county town of Hertford and his body was brought back and hung in chains at nearby Gubblecote as a warning to local people not to take the law into their own hands.

The walk, which is easy and varied in nature, explores the quiet country at the foot of the Chiltern escarpment, taking you first to skirt Wilstone Reservoir before visiting the picturesque Buckinghamshire villages of Drayton Beauchamp and Buckland. Your return route then leads you across fields to join the Aylesbury Arm of the Grand Union Canal for two-thirds of a mile before cutting across a field back into Wilstone.

Starting from Wilstone War Memorial, turn left onto the pavement of the main village street. After 100 yards turn right into Chapel End Lane, keeping left at a fork and continuing past some attractive thatched cottages to the end of the public road. Here take path TR32 straight on along the drive to Church Farm House, soon crossing a stile by a gate and a barn and taking a rough lane straight on. Where the lane turns right, go straight on crossing a stile left of a gate into the left-hand field. Bear slightly left across this field to the corner of a hedge where you bear left and follow the hedge to a footbridge and stile leading to the B489 at a sharp bend. Cross this road and turn left along it, then, at a sharp left-hand bend, step over a crash-barrier and follow a right-hand stream passing right of a fenced car park then climbing a steep bank to reach the edge of Wilstone Reservoir, built in 1802 and enlarged in 1836 and 1839 and a national nature reserve since 1955. (NB If the bank is too slippery, use a flight of steps 60 yards to your left).

Now turn right onto path TR44 along the top of the embankment containing the reservoir with views to your left towards Ivinghoe Beacon and Pitstone Hill, eventually crossing a concrete culvert, entering a belt of poplars and bearing left. Disregard a branching path to your right and continue through the tree-belt for 300 yards to reach a large noticeboard giving details of the birds frequenting the reservoir. Here ignore a handgate and bear slightly right through a fence gap, disregarding a stile in the right-hand fence then crossing a footbridge and stile into a field. Now in Buckinghamshire, take path DB5 bearing half right across the field, passing just left of a sycamore tree at the corner of a hedge and eventually crossing a stile in the far hedge. Here bear half left crossing the next field diagonally and heading for a wooden

63

electricity pylon left of a line of cottages at Drayton Beauchamp to cross two stiles and reach a road. Turn left onto this road then at a left-hand bend turn right through a kissing-gate onto path DB10 bearing left across a field, heading left of the church tower, with views to your left of Upper Farm with its seventeenth-century brick-and-timber farmhouse, to cross a stile by a telegraph pole into Church Lane. Turn right into this lane keeping left at a fork, then cross a stile between gates and take path DB15 bearing slightly left across a field towards a stile in front of two tall trees with a fine view to your left of Drayton Beauchamp Church.

Drayton Beauchamp Church with its chequered stonework was rebuilt in the fifteenth century incorporating many features of its predecessor which is believed to have been twelfth-century. Among its treasures are a Norman font, a rare fifteenth-century ´Creed` window and two fourteenth-century brasses representing Thomas and William Cheyne, lords of the manor of Chelsea, after whose family the famous street called Cheyne Walk in Chelsea is named. Its nineteenth-century pulpit commemorates the brilliant scholar and author of ´Ecclesiastical Polity`, Richard Hooker, who was rector of Drayton Beauchamp from 1584 to 1585 before becoming Master of the Temple in London.

Halfway across the field turn right onto crossing path DB12 to cross a stile into a small plantation in the right-hand corner of the field. Go straight on through the plantation then cross a stile and footbridge and take path B16 straight on across three fields, heading for a flat-topped clump of trees protruding above the skyline left of a group of buildings at Buckland, with views to your left towards Aston Hill and Buckland Wharf, eventually passing through a hedge gap by a white cottage onto Buckland Road. Turn right onto this road to reach the B489 by the former ´Rothschild Arms` at Buckland Crossroads where you take a road straight on into Buckland village.

Having passed Neild´s Farm to your left and Manor Farm to your right, turn right into Peggs Lane, passing the heavily-restored thirteenth-century church with more chequered stonework behind cottages to your left and ignoring a branching path to your left. At a right-hand bend by the entrance to Pound Orchard, turn left onto path B7 passing either side of a gate into a short green lane. Ignore a gate into the churchyard and bear right, crossing a stile by a gate into a field. Go straight on across this field, disregarding the stile of a crossing path in the left-hand hedge and eventually crossing a stile in the far left-hand corner of the field. Now bear left then right following a left-hand hedge to cross two stiles and a footbridge at

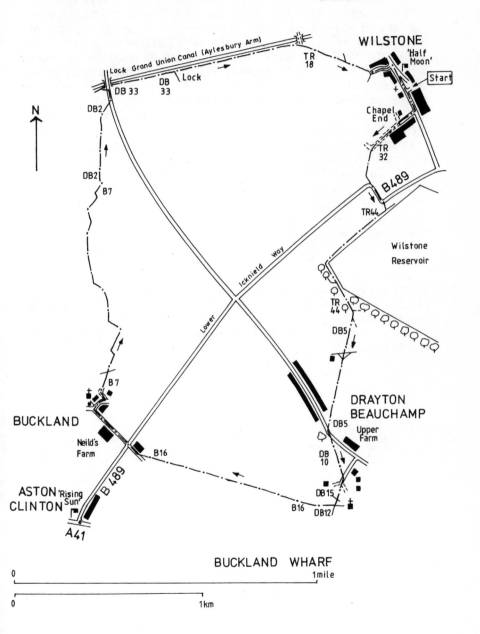

the far side of the field. Here turn left and follow a winding left-hand hedge and stream for half a mile through two fields, ignoring a farm bridge to your left in the second field and eventually, near the far end of the field, turning left over a stile and footbridge. At the far end of the footbridge take path DB2 bearing half right across the field to cross a stile in its far right-hand corner. Now follow a right-hand hedge straight on. Where the hedge bears right, leave it and bear half right across a field corner to cross a footbridge right of a gate and reach the Puttenham road.

Turn left onto this road, then, just before a hump-backed bridge, turn left down a fenced path to a kissing-gate onto path DB33, the towpath of the Aylesbury Arm of the Grand Union Canal, which was built in 1814 to improve access from Aylesbury to the main canal. Turn right onto the towpath passing under the bridge and following it towards the chimneys of the former Pitstone Cement Works and Pitstone Hill for two-thirds of a mile, passing two locks, ignoring a branching path to your right and reentering Hertford-shire. On reaching another canal bridge, bear right leaving the towpath and passing the right-hand end of the bridge parapet, then turn right onto path TR18, soon crossing a stile into a field. Here bear half left, heading for the corner of a hedge left of some indus-trial farm buildings, then follow this left-hand hedge straight on to reach a gate and stile at the end of Sandbrook Lane. Cross the stile and take this road straight on into Wilstone, emerging into the main street almost opposite the ´Half Moon`. Now turn right for your starting point.

WALK 14   Ivinghoe

Length of Walk: (A/B) 4.3 miles / 6.9 Km
Starting Point: ´Rose & Crown`, Ivinghoe.
Grid Ref: SP945163
Maps: OS Landranger Sheet 165
            OS Explorer Sheet 2 (or old Pathfinder Sheet 1094
            (SP81/91))
            Chiltern Society FP Map No.19
How to get there / Parking: Ivinghoe, 3.2 miles northeast of
    Tring, may be reached from the roundabout at the western
    end of the Tring Bypass by taking the B488 towards
    Dunstable for 4.2 miles. On reaching Ivinghoe, ignore the
    B489 to your right, then at a left-hand bend turn right
    into Vicarage Lane to reach the ´Rose & Crown` where
    there are parking bays ahead and to your right.
Notes: The descent from Ivinghoe Beacon on Walk A via path
    IV24 is extremely steep and slippery in wet conditions. If
    wishing to visit the Beacon in such weather, it is therefore
    advisable afterwards to retrace your steps to where the two
    walks fork and continue via Walk B.

Ivinghoe, today best known for the commanding 762ft-high hill
above it called Ivinghoe Beacon with its superb panoramic views,
which serves as the northeastern terminus of the Ridgeway Path,
must, in mediaeval times, have been a settlement of some
importance. The village, near the point where the Ancient British
Icknield Way forks into an upper and lower route, boasts, in particular, a magnificent cruciform church with a copper spire rising
from a central tower built in about 1230 by the Bishop of
Winchester and much altered in the following two centuries and
also a sixteenth-century town hall now used as a library which
confirms that Ivinghoe was then considered a town. Also of
interest is the thatch-hook on the churchyard wall used for drag-
ging burning thatch off cottage roofs to prevent fires spreading.
Other fine buildings in Ivinghoe include the ´King´s Head`, a
fifteenth-century inn largely rebuilt in the seventeenth century
and the eighteenth-century Old Brewery House, now used as a
youth hostel, while, in 1820, the novelist Sir Walter Scott made
the village famous by adapting its name for the title of his novel

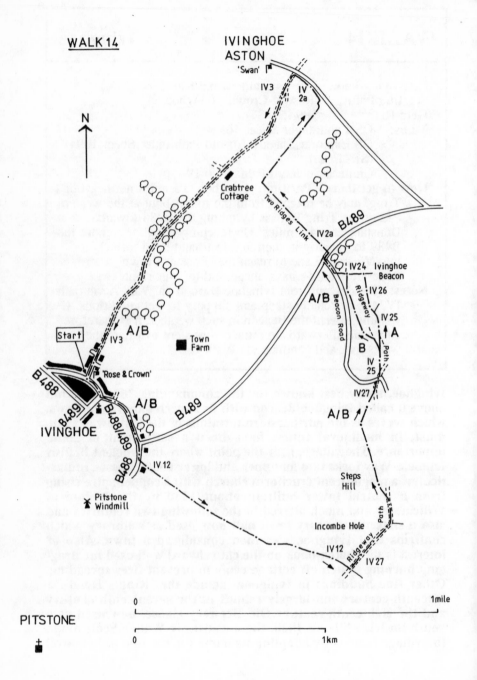

WALK 14

IVINGHOE
ASTON

'Swan'

IV3

IV
2a

Crabtree
Cottage

Two Ridges Link

B489

IV 2a

IV24 Ivinghoe
Beacon

IV 26

A/B

Beacon Road

Ridgeway

IV 25

Start

IV3

A/B

Town
Farm

A

B

IV
25

'Rose & Crown'

B488

A/B

IV27

IVINGHOE

B489

B488/489

B489

A/B

Steps
Hill

IV 12

Path

Pitstone
Windmill

Incombe Hole

IV 12

IV27

Ridgeway

Path

N

0   1mile

0   1km

PITSTONE

'Ivanhoe`.

The walk takes you from the village to explore the Ivinghoe Hills with their superb views with an optional visit to the top of Ivinghoe Beacon. You then descend to the edge of Ivinghoe Aston before taking an ancient green lane back into Ivinghoe.

Both walks start from the 'Rose & Crown`, Ivinghoe and take Vicarage Lane southeastwards to reach the B488/B489 opposite the church. Turn left onto its nearside footway, soon with fine views to your right towards Pitstone Windmill, one of the oldest surviving postmills in England dating from 1627, restored by the National Trust, and the disused Pitstone Cement Works. At the road junction where the ancient Icknield Way is said to have forked, go straight on, crossing the B489 and taking the B488 towards Tring. Just before the second bungalow to your left, turn left over low rails by a gate and take fenced path IV12 with views to your left towards Ivinghoe Beacon and Steps Hill. On emerging over a low rail into a field, follow the left-hand hedge straight on for a quarter mile climbing gently with fine views to your right towards Pitstone Hill, Pitstone's thirteenth-century church with a fifteenth-century tower backed by Aston Hill and the cement works. Where the hedge turns left, take what is normally a crop-break straight on, gradually bearing left with close-up views of Ivinghoe Beacon and Steps Hill, passing the end of a hedge to your left and going through a gap in a second hedge. Here bear slightly left heading for a stile in a fence on the next rise, passing a deep, steep-sided coombe to your left called Incombe Hole. Having crossed the stile, where there is also a fine view behind you towards Ivinghoe and Mentmore Towers, built by Sir Joseph Paxton, designer of the Crystal Palace, for Baron de Rothschild in 1852 and later home to his son-in-law and one-time prime minister, the fifth Earl of Rosebery, turn right and follow the right-hand fence to a gate and kissing-gate in the fence.

Here turn left onto the Ridgeway Path (IV27) with superb views in all directions, soon passing the left-hand end of a sporadic hedge and joining a chalky track which you follow round the top of Incombe Hole, ignoring a branching path to your right and climbing to a gate and stile. Do **NOT** cross the stile but pass left of it along the top edge of Incombe Hole, then bear slightly right across open downland into a belt of scrub. On reemerging with fine views ahead towards Ivinghoe Beacon and across the Vale of Aylesbury towards Leighton Buzzard, ignore a stile to your right and follow the right-hand fence downhill to a corner where you cross a stile, bear half right over a rise and then descend, ignoring a path merg-

69

ing from your right to reach a bend in Beacon Road at the top of the ´pass`. Cross this road and bear half left between wooden bollards onto chalky downland path IV25 over a slight rise.

Where the path bears left, **Walk A** leaves it and goes straight on across the grass to join a parallel chalky track passing right of a hillock. At a waymarked fork keep left, taking path IV26 steeply uphill to the cairn at the top of Ivinghoe Beacon. Having stopped to enjoy the superb panorama, turn sharp left onto path IV24 to reach the left-hand end of a fence where you descend extremely steeply to reach Beacon Road just left of a cattle grid. (NB If the descent is too wet and slippery, retrace your steps to the slight rise, then take Walk B).

Walk B continues along the path for another 80 yards and then forks left onto a worn path entering a sunken way right of a deep earthwork and following it with fine views ahead later with Beacon Road to your left. On reaching a steep eroded slope, fork right onto a path behind some hawthorn bushes and continue parallel to the road until you reach crossing path IV24 near a clump of Scots pines. Turn left onto this to reach the road just left of a cattle grid.

Both walks now turn right onto Beacon Road passing through a gate right of the cattle grid to reach the B489. Cross this fast road carefully and turn right onto its footway. After 40 yards turn left over a stile onto path IV2a (part of the Two Ridges Link) and follow a left-hand hedge downhill with fine views ahead towards Ivinghoe Aston, Slapton and Leighton Buzzard and to your right towards Edlesborough with its prominent fourteenth-century church with a massive tower famous for its fifteenth-century wood-work, Eaton Bray and Totternhoe. At the bottom end of the field go through a kissing-gate and follow a left-hand fence straight on over a rise passing an old chalk quarry to your right, then, at the bottom left-hand corner of the field turn right and follow a left-hand fence to the far side of the field. Here ignore a gate ahead and turn left through a kissing-gate, then turn right rounding a corner of the field and following the back of a roadside hedge downhill to a kissing-gate leading to the point where bridleway IV3, an ancient green road, possibly a continuation of the Lower Icknield Way, crosses the road into Ivinghoe Aston. Turn left onto the bridleway, following a macadam drive at first. Where the drive wiggles to the left, leave it and take a hedged green lane straight on for a mile, ignoring branching tracks to right and left, passing through a copse and eventually reaching the end of a road in Ivinghoe where your starting point is straight ahead.

70

WALK 15   Tring Station

Length of Walk: 4.1 miles / 6.6 Km
Starting Point: Entrance to Tring Station.
Grid Ref: SP951123
Maps: OS Landranger Sheet 165
OS Explorer Sheet 2 (or old Pathfinder Sheet 1094 (SP81/91))
Chiltern Society FP Map No.19
How to get there / Parking: Tring Station, 1.7 miles northeast of the centre of Tring, may be reached from the town by taking the road signposted to Tring Station and Aldbury to Tring Station where you pass the station and cross the railway bridge and the station car park is on your right. On-street parking near the station is also possible except on weekday mornings.
Notes: Heavy nettle growth may be encountered on bridleway AB56 in the summer months and path AB60 may be diverted to pass left of the school playing field.

Tring Station, on the L&NWR Euston-Birmingham main line, built in 1838 and now known as the West Coast main line, was, like many Victorian railway stations, some distance from the settlement it served and indeed was so far from the town as to be in the neighbouring parish of Aldbury, which this walk explores.

Aldbury village, which you visit in the course of the walk, is a renowned picture-postcard village with a green with a duckpond, stocks and a whipping-post surrounded by attractive sixteenth- and seventeenth-century cottages and a seventeenth-century manor house. The nearby church, of thirteenth-century origin but now mainly fourteenth-century with a fifteenth-century tower, is noted for its monuments to the Duncombe family who held Stocks Manor for 500 years and the Pendley Chapel with its monuments to the Whittingham and Verney families and a fine stone screen, which were moved to the church from the former Ashridge Monastery in 1575. Buried in the churchyard is Mrs. Humphrey Ward (1851 -1920), a grand-daughter of Dr. Arnold of Rugby School, a niece of the poet Matthew Arnold and a popular novelist of her day, whose husband bought Stocks in the 1890s and who was visited there by her son-in-law, the historian

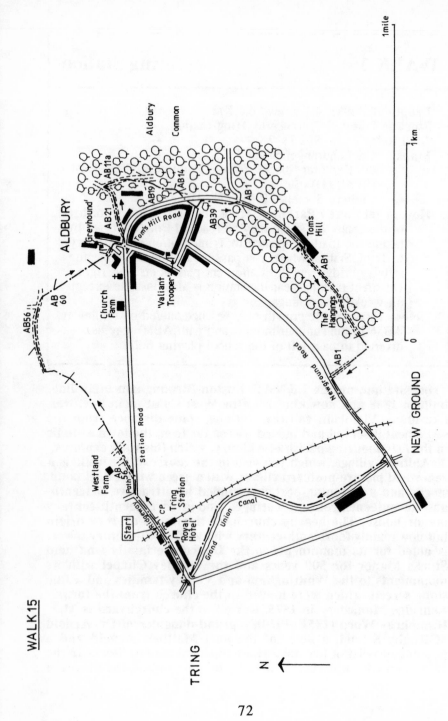

WALK15

72

Dr. G.M. Trevelyan and the playwright George Bernard Shaw.

The walk, which includes a series of fine views, leads you from Tring Station to the picturesque village of Aldbury before skirting its wooded common and climbing to Tom's Hill. You then descend to reach the tranquil sylvan towpath of the Grand Union Canal, which you follow back to the station.

Starting from the entrance to Tring Station, cross Station Road and turn right onto its far pavement. At its junction with Northfield Road go straight on for a further 100 yards, then fork left through a bridlegate beside a cattle grid onto bridleway AB56, part of the Ridgeway Path, following a concrete drive. Where the drive turns left through a gate, leave it and take a grassy track straight on to a bridlegate leading to a signposted crossways. Here, leaving the Ridgeway Path, go straight on through a bridlegate and take a fenced bridleway to another bridlegate where you ignore a branching bridleway to your left and keep straight on, now with a golf course to your left. Where the fenced bridleway transfers to the other side of the hedge, a fine view briefly opens out to your right towards Aldbury backed by the wooded hill of Aldbury Common with the top of the Bridgewater Monument, built in 1832 in memory of the canal-building third Duke of Bridgewater of nearby Ashridge, protruding above the treetops left of the village.

On reaching a crossing path, go straight on for a further third of a mile, soon with hedges on both sides, ignoring a branching path and field gate to your left, then looking out for a hedge gap to your right leading to a concealed stile. Turn right here onto path AB60, crossing the stile and bearing half left across a field to a corner of a hedge where a fine view of Aldbury opens out ahead. Here keep straight on to pass just left of the more distant of two electricity poles and cross a stile just left of the corner of a fence, then bear half left, crossing a playing field diagonally to a stile by the right-hand end of a long red-brick building. Now go straight on down a macadam drive to reach Aldbury village green.

Continue to the far side of the green, then turn right onto a road left of the green and pond to reach a crossroads. Here turn left into Tom's Hill Road. After 60 yards fork left onto bridleway AB21, a rough lane climbing into the woods of Aldbury Common where it becomes steeper. On reaching a clearing, turn sharp right onto bridleway AB11a. Where this divides into lower and upper paths, take the right-hand (upper) path beside garden fences. Where the fences end, ignore a crossing path, then some 25 yards further on, fork right onto ill-defined bridleway AB19 through the woods. On reaching a power line, bear half left along the right-hand side of its clearing, entering further woodland and crossing an overgrown sunken way, then, at a fork, take the right-hand option (bridleway AB14) straight on, dropping steeply into a sunken way. Here at a five-way junction bear half right into a branching sunken way to reach Tom's Hill Road. Cross this and go straight on to reach the end of Malting Lane on the edge of Aldbury.

Here turn left onto path AB39 climbing steeply past a seat into woodland and continuing less steeply uphill, ignoring a minor crossing path. On nearing Tom's Hill Road, keep right at a fork to join the road by the end of a crash-barrier. Turn right onto this road, then at a junction where the major road bears left, take the branching road (byway AB1) straight on, ignoring a branching bridleway to your right and branching footpath to your left. Where the macadam road forks, take the right-hand option straight on, disregarding another branching path to your right. Just past Rose Cottage, fork right onto a rough track through a gate right of a wooden barn, following a right-hand fence to a gate into a field. Now follow a left-hand hedge straight on, passing through the right-hand of two gates and a further gate to enter a wood called The Hangings. Descend gradually through this, passing through two more gates to enter a field where a fine view opens out ahead across the Tring Gap towards Wigginton and the spectacular Ridgeway Path footbridge over the new A41. Go straight on across this field to its far hedge, then turn right and follow this sporadic left-hand hedge downhill through two fields, with a fine view to your right towards Aldbury backed by Clipper Down and the Bridgewater Monument, to reach gates onto Newground Road.

Turn left onto this road and follow it for a third of a mile, ignoring a branching bridleway to your left and crossing a bridge over the railway. On reaching a bridge over the Grand Union Canal, built as the Grand Junction Canal between 1793 and 1806 by the third Duke of Bridgewater and his engineer friend James Brindley to improve freight transport between London and the industrial Midlands and North in the days before the railways had been conceived of and only renamed in 1929, turn right through a hedge gap by the start of its right-hand parapet and descend a slope to join the towpath. Now follow this towpath straight on through a quiet tree-lined and hand-dug cutting for nearly a mile to reach the modern bridge over the canal bearing Station Road. Go under this bridge then turn sharp right up a flight of steps to reach the road where you turn left for your starting point.

WALK 16   Berkhamsted (Bank Mill)

Length of Walk: 5.1 miles / 8.2 Km
Starting Point: Junction of Bullbeggars Lane and Bank Mill Lane on the edge of Berkhamsted.
Grid Ref: TL006071
Maps: OS Landranger Sheet 166
OS Pathfinder Sheet 1119 (TL00/10)
Chiltern Society FP Maps Nos. 5, 17 & 20
How to get there / Parking: Bank Mill, 0.8 miles southeast of the centre of Berkhamsted, may be reached from the town by taking the A4251 towards Hemel Hempstead. On nearing the edge of the town, turn left into Bullbeggars Lane, where you can park in a large parking area on your left at its junction with Bank Mill Lane.
Notes: Garden Field Lane is prone to heavy nettle growth in the summer months.

Berkhamsted, locally pronounced ´Berk´msted` in the narrow Bulbourne valley from London through the Chilterns to the Tring Gap and the Midlands beyond, has always been a place of transit. The Romans constructed Akeman Street through the town, which has now become the A4251. William the Conqueror passed through Berkhamsted in 1066 on his circuitous progression from the Battle of Hastings to London and it was here that he accepted the Saxon surrender. He also gave the manor to his half-brother, Robert of Mortain, who built a castle here to protect London from attack from the northwest. With the coming of the Industrial Revolution requiring improved freight transport links between London and the industrial Midlands and North, it was through Berkhamsted that the third Duke of Bridgewater of nearby Ashridge and his engineer friend James Brindley built the Grand Junction Canal in the 1790s (since 1929 called the Grand Union Canal) and this was followed in 1838 by the L&NWR main line from Euston to Birmingham which even involved demolishing the Norman castle gates. However, although the M1 gave some temporary relief to Akeman Street, it was not till 1993 that the long-planned A41 bypass was built to relieve the town of its horrendous through-traffic.

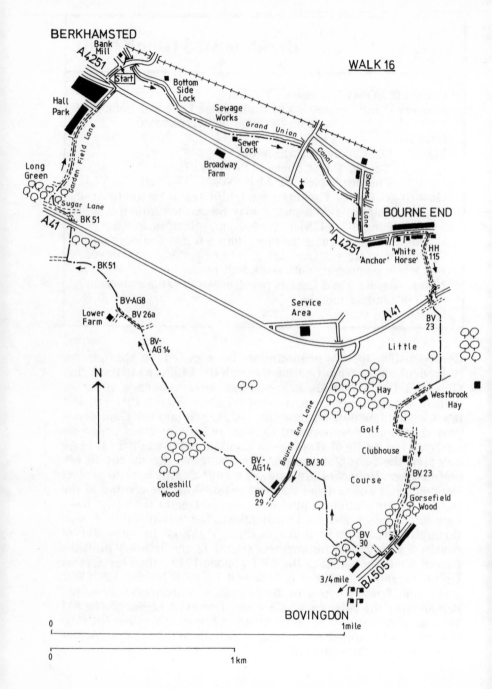

BERKHAMSTED

Bank Mill

A 4251

Start

Hall Park

Long Green

Sugar Lane

BK 51

A41

BK 51

Lower Farm

BV-AG8

BV 26a

BV-AG 14

N

Coleshill Wood

BV-AG14

BV 29

Garden Field Lane

Bottom Side Lock

Sewage Works

Grand Union

Sewer Lock

Broadway Farm

Canal

Sharpes Lane

BOURNE END

A4251

'Anchor'

'White Horse'

HH 115

Service Area

A41

BV 23

Little

Hay

Westbrook Hay

Golf

Clubhouse

BV 23

Course

Gorsefield Wood

Bourne End Lane

BV 30

BV 30

3/4 mile

B4505

BOVINGDON

WALK 16

0   1mile

0   1 km

76

The walk, which is inevitably coloured in places by these transport links, starts at Bank Mill on the old River Bulbourne and first follows the pleasant canal towpath, occasionally disturbed by a passing train, to reach Bourne End with its coaching inns astride Akeman Street. You then cross the bypass and climb to the Bovingdon ridge with its superb views across the Bulbourne valley and surrounding hills before crossing the pleasant branching valley of a seasonal stream called Bourne Gutter and another ridge to return to your starting point.

Starting from the junction of Bullbeggars Lane and Bank Mill Lane on the edge of Berkhamsted, take the continuation of Bullbeggars Lane eastwards. Before reaching Bank Mill Bridge over the Grand Union Canal, fork left onto a path beside a left-hand hedge leading to the canal towpath. Turn right onto the towpath passing under Bank Mill Bridge, following the canal for nearly a mile past Bottom Side Lock and, now with the River Bulbourne to your right, Sewer Lock and passing under bridge no.145, soon with views to your right of Bourne End Church, built in 1854 by Sir George Gilbert Scott, architect of the famous neo-gothic Midland Grand Hotel in front of St. Pancras Station. On nearing bridge no.146, turn right up a slope into Sharpes Lane and follow it straight on for 220 yards, soon crossing the River Bulbourne and reaching the A4251 at Bourne End.

Turn left onto its nearside footway, then, where it ends, cross the main road and continue along its right-hand footway, crossing Bourne End Lane and passing the ´Anchor` and ´White Horse`. At the end of the right-hand footway turn right onto byway HH115, following a green lane gently uphill, crossing a stile by a gate and taking a fenced bridleway bearing left then right to reach a bridge over the A41 where there are fine views behind you up the Bulbourne valley towards Berkhamsted and to your right across the suburbs of Hemel Hempstead. At the far end of the bridge take path BV23 straight on. At the edge of Little Hay Golf Course by a small tree and a litter bin, bear slightly right uphill to pass just left of a small copse on the skyline with views to your left of Westbrook Hay, a nineteenth-century mansion which, at one time, housed the postwar Hemel Hempstead New Town Development Corporation.

Having passed the copse, continue to a stunted oak tree at the back edge of the golf course, then turn right and follow a left-hand fence at first, later continuing along a grassy track passing two bungalows to your left and a series of rustic seats to your right with fine views up the Bulbourne valley towards Berkhamsted. On reaching a corner of a hedge, bear half left following the hedge to join a macadam drive by a barn. Now take this drive bearing left round the back of the barn and later right to pass the clubhouse and car park. On reaching a corner of Gorsefield Wood, at a road hump bear slightly left onto a path into the wood (still BV23), later ignoring a parallel bridleway to your left, crossing a stile by a gate and bearing slightly left to reach the B4505 on the edge of Bovingdon.

Turn right onto its nearside footway, then after 150 yards cross the entrance to the Little Hay Golf Complex and take fenced bridleway BV30 along the back of the B4505 hedge. Now follow this winding fenced bridleway around the edge of the golf course for over half a mile, eventually passing through a hedge gap into Bourne End Lane. Turn left onto this road, soon passing two bungalows, then, at the end of the public road where there is a gate ahead, turn right over a stile onto path BV29 (later BV-AG14) following a right-hand hedge. At the far end of the field turn right through a hedge gap then left and follow the edge of the field down a valley bottom, passing a copse and part of Coleshill Wood. At the bottom corner of the field cross a stile and bear half right along what is normally a crop break over the top of a rise then dropping to the end of a hedge, which you follow downhill to a gate and stile onto a farm road in the Bourne Gutter valley.

Bear slightly left onto this farm road (path BV26a), then, where it bears left towards Lower Farm, leave it and take bridleway BV-AG8 straight on, soon turning right through a bridlegate and following a left-hand hedge. Where the hedge bears left, leave it and take bridleway BK51 straight on across the field to join a barbed-wire fence, which you follow to a bridlegate and signpost. Turn right through this gate and take path BK51, following a right-hand hedge uphill past a copse then continuing to a stile into an A41 underpass. At the far end of the underpass bear left up a slope to a squeeze-stile into Sugar Lane, then take this rough lane straight on into woodland at Long Green. Just inside the woods turn right onto a permissive path, then at a T-junction turn right again. At the far side of the wood go straight on into Garden Field Lane and take this narrow flint lane for over a third of a mile over a slight rise and then downhill, passing the Hall Park estate to your left, where you ignore branching paths to your left, and continuing to the A4251. Cross this main road and turn left onto its far footway, then turn right into Bullbeggars Lane for your starting point.

WALK 17   Berkhamsted Common

Length of Walk: 3.8 miles / 6.2 Km
Starting Point: Road junction by the war memorial on
                      Berkhamsted Common.
Grid Ref: TL005092
Maps: OS Landranger Sheets 165 & 166
            OS Pathfinder Sheets 1095 (TL01/11) & 1119
            (TL00/10) & Explorer Sheet 2 (or old Pathfinder
            Sheets 1094 (SP81/91) & 1118 (SP80/90))
            Chiltern Society FP Maps 19 & 20
How to get there / Parking: Berkhamsted Common, on the
    plateau north of the town, may be reached from the
    junction of the A416 & A4251 in the town centre by
    taking the road signposted to Potten End. By the station
    turn left under the railway and continue to follow signs
    for Potten End and Ashridge for just over a mile to reach
    the woods on Berkhamsted Common. At the T-junction
    by the war memorial turn left then immediately left again
    into a small car park.

Berkhamsted Common with its extensive woodland is today taken
for granted as a place where local people and Londoners can go
for fresh air and exercise, but few of its many visitors realise that
in 1866 it was all but lost to land enclosure. In that year 400
acres of the Common, which had in mediaeval times formed part
of the park of Berkhamsted´s Norman castle, were enclosed by
the lord of the manor, Lord Brownlow of Ashridge Park with a
high iron fence. This might easily have led to the land being split
into fields and brought into agricultural use, but Augustus Smith,
owner of the nearby Ashlyns Estate and one of the enraged
Berkhamsted commoners, supported by Lord Eversley, chairman
of the newly-founded Commons Preservation Society (now
renamed as the Open Spaces Society), assembled a gang of 100
London labourers and chartered a special train to bring them by
dead of night to Berkhamsted Common. By 6 a.m. the fence had
been completely dismantled and four years of litigation followed,
but finally in 1870 Augustus Smith won with an injunction being
granted forbidding enclosure and defining the rights of common.
This judgment did not, of course, give public access but preserved

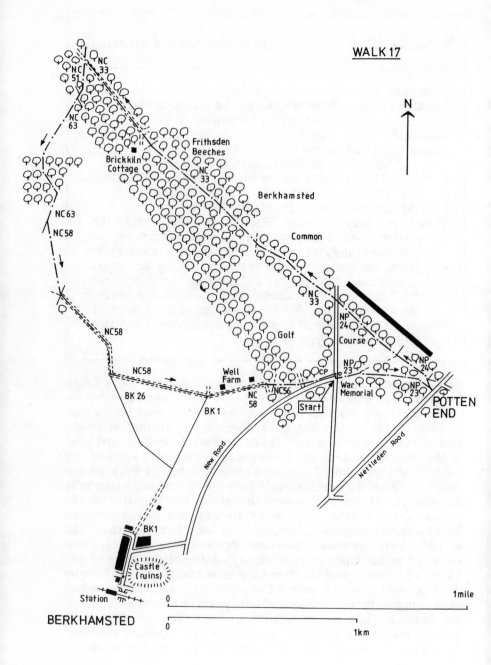

N

NC 51
NC 33

NC 63

Frithsden Beeches

Brickkiln Cottage

NC 33

Berkhamsted

NC 63

NC 58

Common

NC 58

NC 33

NP 24

Golf

Course

NP 24

NC 58

CP

NP 23

Well Farm

NP 23

BK 26

War Memorial

NC 56

BK 1

NC 58

Start

POTTEN END

BK 1

New Road

Nettleden Road

Castle (ruins)

BK 1

Station

0   1mile

0   1km

BERKHAMSTED

80

the rights of common so that when the Law of Property Act 1925 granted public access to urban commons, Berkhamsted Common was able to qualify, subject to certain limitations to protect the golf course.

The walk first explores part of the common where tracts of woodland are interspersed with golf course fairways and areas of scrub before emerging from the woods, crossing a valley to reach Castle Hill with its fine views across the town and returning to your starting point.

Starting from the road junction by the war memorial on Berkhamsted Common, take bridleway NP23 along a gravel track passing right of the memorial to the men of the Inns of Court Regiment who trained on the Common in the First World War and soon crossing a fairway where you look out for balls driven from your right. Now go straight on through a belt of trees to a second fairway where beware of balls driven from your left. Here keep straight on into a further belt of trees where you keep left at a fork and ignore a crossing track to reach a third fairway with balls driven from your right. At the far side go straight on through woodland to reach a clearing by Nettleden Road on the edge of Potten End.

Do NOT join this road but turn sharp left onto bridleway NP24, reentering the woodland and ignoring a branching path to your right. On emerging by a tee, pass left of it, then bear slightly right across the fairway aiming for a prominent silver birch tree on its right-hand edge. Here disregard a path signposted to your right and take a worn path straight on past the birch tree into woodland where you continue parallel to the fairway passing a green and eventually reaching the road to Ashridge. Cross this road and take bridleway NC33 straight on through a belt of trees to reach another fairway where balls are driven from your left. Keep straight on crossing the fairway at an angle and passing left of some mounds to reach a waymarking post. Here bear slightly left onto a wide track into a belt of trees, walking parallel to a right-hand fairway, ignoring a crossing golfers´ path, then continuing past a green. Keep straight on through the trees for some distance, eventually emerging by a further green to your right. Here ignore a crossing golfers´ path and go straight on across the wooded common, leaving the golf course behind.

On reaching a waymarked crossways, take bridleway NC33 straight on passing right of two small oak trees. After a further third of a mile at a track junction by the corner of an open field to your right and buildings to your left, again take bridleway NC33 straight on through the trees parallel to the field edge to your right. After a further third of a mile at a waymarked crossways, turn sharp left onto bridleway NC51, eventually reaching a waymarked fork near the edge of the wood. Here fork right onto path NC63 crossing a stile and following a right-hand hedge straight on through two fields to a stile into a wood and the Alpine Meadow Nature Reserve. Bear slightly left and follow an obvious path downhill through the wood and a large grassy clearing then up again to cross a stile into a field. Now turn right following a right-hand hedge uphill to cross a stile by a gate, then take path NC58 bearing half left and crossing a field diagonally to its far corner.

Here bear left, taking a grassy track left of an old gate and following a right-hand hedge along the top of Castle Hill through two fields with views across Berkhamsted to your right in places. In the second field, on reaching a corner where a gate and stile ahead give a fine view across the town, turn left and continue to follow the grassy track downhill through two fields to a crossways near Well Farm. Here ignore a crossing track and take a fenced track (still path NC58) uphill past the farm, joining a macadam drive by a bungalow. Where the drive bears right, leave it and go straight on over a stile into woodland on Berkhamsted Common. Now take bridleway NC56 straight on, ignoring branching paths to right and left, until you reach a crossing stone track near New Road to your right. Here take a permissive bridleway straight on parallel to the road to reach the back of the car park near your starting point.

WALK 18   Great Gaddesden

Length of Walk: 5.0 miles / 8.1 Km
Starting Point: 'Cock & Bottle`, Great Gaddesden.
Grid Ref: TL030112
Maps: OS Landranger Sheet 166
OS Pathfinder Sheet 1095 (TL01/11)
Chiltern Society FP Map No.20
How to get there / Parking: Great Gaddesden, 3 miles north-west of Hemel Hempstead, may be reached from the town by taking the A4146 towards Leighton Buzzard. Having passed through Water End, at the next crossroads turn left onto Pipers Hill for Great Gaddesden. Just before the 'Cock & Bottle` turn right into Church Meadow and find a suitable place to park. Do **not** use the pub car park without the landlord's permission.

Great Gaddesden, which, like so many other 'great` villages, is smaller than the 'little` village of the same name, is set in an idyllic location in the Gade valley, but the picturesque cluster of church, farm, inn, school and cottages is marred by an insensitive council house development tacked onto it. In the past Great Gaddesden was very much the estate village of the Halseys who have lived here since 1512, still have a large estate here and continue to live at Gaddesden Place on a hilltop above the valley. This Palladian mansion was built for the Halseys between 1768 and 1773 by James Wyatt, designer of Ashridge, to replace their previous house, the Golden Parsonage near Gaddesden Row, of which only a wing from 1705 remains, while the church contains the eighteenth-century Halsey Chapel with over twenty monuments to family members including examples of the work of Rysbrack and Flaxman. The twelfth-century church is also noted for the use of Roman bricks from a nearby villa in its construction and its massive fifteenth-century tower with some fearsome gargoyles.

The walk leads you from the village up through Hoo Wood to explore the quiet upland plateau around Jockey End. Your somewhat longer return route takes you by way of the Halseys' estate passing close to the Golden Parsonage and Gaddesden Place before descending with fine views into Great Gaddesden.

WALK 18

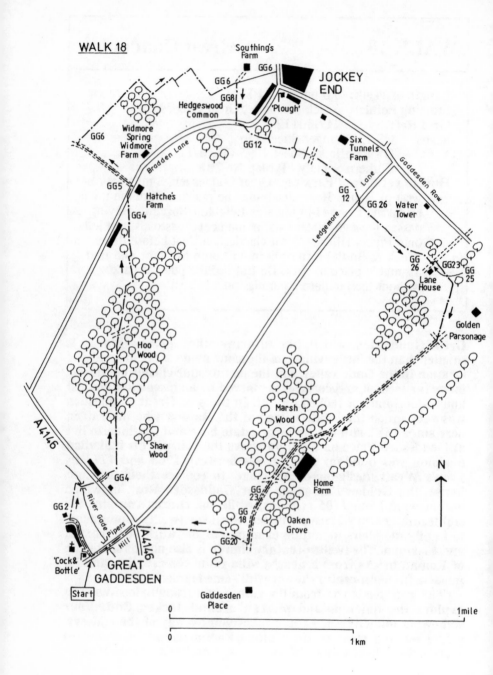

84

Starting from the 'Cock & Bottle' in Great Gaddesden, take Church Meadow ignoring a fork to your left. Where the road bears left near a children's playground, leave it and go straight on towards the playground, then turn right over a stile onto path GG2 bearing left across a meadow to another stile by the corner of a hedge. Now bear half right across the next meadow passing just left of two backwaters of the River Gade then turning sharp right to cross the marshy river by a causeway and footbridges and continue across a field to a stile onto the A4146. Cross this main road carefully and take path GG4 straight on up a concrete drive to a car park. Here follow the right-hand hedge straight on, soon bearing left. Where the hedge bears right, leave it and go straight on uphill across the field to a concealed stile into Hoo Wood. At a waymarked fork in the wood, take the left-hand option straight on and follow the obvious, if at times overgrown, path straight on through the wood for half a mile, ignoring a branching path to your right and a wide crossing track, eventually passing through a broken kissing-gate and crossing a stile to enter a field. Here bear right following a thick right-hand hedge to a former gateway in it. Go through this and continue along the other side of the hedge past a copse to cross a stile by a gate in a field corner. Now follow a right-hand hedge straight on to a gate and stile into Bradden Lane near Hatche's Farm with its striking converted weatherboarded barns.

Turn right onto this road and follow it uphill. By the entrance to Hatche's Barn, turn left onto byway GG5 along a rough hedged lane, ignoring a branching track to your left. Where the right-hand hedge ends, take the lane's fenced grassy continuation straight on until it bears left towards an iron gate. Here turn right over a stile onto path GG6 heading for the left-hand corner of a wood called Widmore Spring, then follow the outside edge of the wood straight on to the far end of the field. Now cross a concealed rail-stile and turn right along the edge of the wood to a field corner. Here turn left and follow a right-hand hedge for 150 yards to a gate and stile in it. Turn right over the stile then left and follow the other side of the hedge to a field corner where you turn right, still following the left-hand hedge. Where the hedge turns left, continue to follow it. At the next field corner turn right onto path GG8 following a left-hand hedge to another corner where you go straight on through a hedge gap into Gaddesden Row cricket field and follow its left-hand hedge to rejoin Bradden Lane on the edge of Jockey End.

Turn left onto this road, then, just before a left-hand bend, turn right through an old gateway onto path GG12 following a left-hand hedge. Where this hedge bears left, bear half right along what is normally a crop-break to a corner of another hedge, then bear half left beside this hedge. Where the hedge turns right, bear half left across the field, walking parallel to a powerline to a corner of another hedge by a cherry tree. Here bear half right and follow the left-hand hedge straight on through two fields, crossing a stile. In the second field, ignore the gate and stile of a crossing path and continue to the far side of the field. Here keep straight on past a disused stile, crossing a farm track and a stile and then continuing across a field to a stile right of an oak tree. Now follow a left-hand fence straight on into the bottom of a dip where you bear slightly right to cross a stile in the top hedge leading to Ledgemore Lane.

Turn right onto this road, then immediately left over a stile onto path GG26 straight across the field with a view of Gaddesden Row water-tower to your left, passing just right of two oak trees to cross two stiles between oak trees in the next hedge. Now keep straight on to a stile in a fenceline, then bear slightly left to a further stile near a corner of a copse. Follow the fenced path past the copse crossing another stile and continuing past a duckpond to reach the drive to the seventeenth-century timber-framed Lane House. Turn left onto this drive (path GG25), then immediately right over a stile onto path GG23 following a right-hand hedge to the far side of the field. Here turn right over one stile then left over two more with a view of the Golden Parsonage opening out ahead. Now bear half right crossing two fields diagonally to a hedge gap on a farm road. Bear half right onto this farm road, where there are fine views of the Golden Parsonage behind you, ignoring a crossing track and following a right-hand hedge for half a mile towards Home Farm.

At a corner of Marsh Wood, fork right onto a track between gateposts in the wood. Take this track straight on through the wood, ignoring a branching track to your right and passing the back of Home Farm, then ignoring a crossing track and continuing to a gate into a field where a fine view opens out across the Gade valley towards Ashridge. Here continue, ignoring a crossing track, going through another gate and passing left of an oak tree. Now take a grassy track, gradually swinging left and becoming path GG18 to reach a gate and stile where Gaddesden Place is ahead. Do **not** cross this stile (unless wishing to take a look at Gaddesden Place), but turn right onto path GG20, following a left-hand fence downhill with fine views ahead towards Great Gaddesden. Having crossed two stiles, go straight on downhill across a field to gates and a stile in the bottom corner leading to Great Gaddesden crossroads. Here cross the A4146 carefully and take Pipers Hill straight on, crossing a bridge over the River Gade to reach your starting point.

WALK 19　　　　　　　　　　Piccott´s End

Length of Walk: 4.9 miles / 8.0 Km
Starting Point: ´Boars Head`, Piccott´s End.
Grid Ref: TL053089
Maps: OS Landranger Sheet 166
　　　OS Pathfinder Sheets 1095 (TL01/11) &
　　　1119 (TL00/10)
　　　(part only) Chiltern Society FP Map No.20
How to get there / Parking: Piccott´s End, on the northern edge of Hemel Hempstead, may be reached from the town centre by taking the A4146 towards Leighton Buzzard to the roundabout at its junction with the A4147. Here turn right onto the A4147, then, at the next roundabout, turn left onto the road into Piccott´s End and follow it for 300 yards to the ´Boars Head` where on-street parking is possible. Do **not** use the pub car park without the landlord´s permission.
Notes: Heavy nettle growth may be encountered on path HH12 in the summer months.

Piccott´s End, on the River Gade only a mile north of the centre of Hemel Hempstead, is still an attractive village in a relatively unspoilt setting despite the fact that the town´s rapidly expanding housing estates have covered the tops of the hills on either side of the valley. In 1953 mediaeval wall-paintings were discovered in a fifteenth-century cottage in the village called Hall House, which also has a priest hide and a mediaeval well.

The walk, which offers superb views across the Gade valley and surrounding hills in places, first leads you up a disused country lane towards the suburb of Grovehill before turning northeast past the edge of this estate to reach Dodds Lane. You then explore the quiet upland plateau on the east side of the Gade valley, passing the tiny hamlet of Lovetts End before eventually descending into the Gade valley at Water End, crossing the valley and turning south past the part sixteenth-century Gaddesden Hall to return to Piccott´s End.

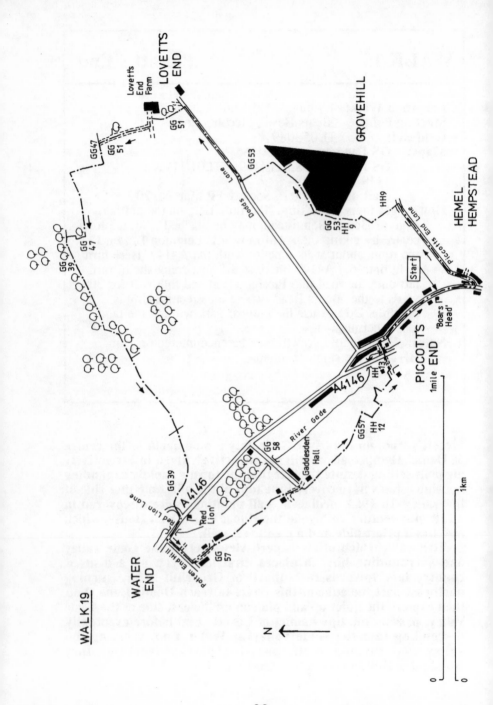

WALK 19

88

Starting from the 'Boars Head', Piccott's End, take the main village street southwards for 200 yards, then, just before the 'Marchmont Arms', turn left into Piccott's End Lane. Now ignore a branching path to your right and at the edge of the village, go straight on through a gap beside a padlocked gate and continue uphill along the lane (now a footpath and cycle track) for a quarter mile. On starting to descend into a slight dip, at the far end of a large gap in the left-hand hedge, turn left onto path HH9 following a right-hand hedge uphill with views across the Gade valley opening out to your left. Near the top of the hill ignore a gap in the right-hand hedge, then bear right, continuing to follow the right-hand hedge, soon on path GG53. At the far side of the field disregard a branching path to your left and bear slightly right, following the right-hand hedge through a second field to the third pair of wooden pylons to your left. Here turn left across the field to reach an unfenced road called Dodds Lane by a telegraph pole right of one with a prop.

Turn right onto this quiet road and follow it for nearly a third of a mile. Just before the entrance to Lovetts End Farm, turn left onto path GG51, following a right-hand hedge to gates into the farm. Here turn left onto a grassy track, then immediately right onto another grassy track (bridleway GG51) following a right-hand hedge. Where the hedge ends, ignore a stile to your right and take the track straight on beside a right-hand fence to a hedge gap under an oak tree. Go through this and turn left onto bridleway GG47, following a left-hand hedge to a corner of the field. Here go straight on through a wide hedge gap then turn right and follow a right-hand hedge round the edge of a large field, turning left at the first corner and later right, then right again, then left to reach a T-junction with bridleway GG39 under an oak tree with a holly hedge in front of you.

Now turn left onto bridleway GG39, still following a right-hand hedge for a further third of a mile, passing through a copse at one point and continuing to the corner of a second copse. Here go straight on through a hedge gap and take a fenced bridleway along the edge of the copse with fine views opening out ahead across the Gade valley towards Nettleden and Ashridge. Where the enclosing fence ends, follow the left-hand hedge straight on downhill ignoring a branching path to your left. At the bottom of a dip, where the left-hand hedge ends, disregard a crossing path and take bridleway GG39 straight on for a quarter mile, following the right-hand hedge over a rise and then downhill towards Water End to reach Red Lion Lane. Turn left onto this road to meet the A4146 virtually opposite the 'Red Lion' at Water End.

Cross this main road carefully and turn right onto its footway to cross a bridge over the River Gade. Now turn left into Potten End Hill and after 200 yards turn left again into Willows Lane (path GG57). Take this rough road to cross a stile by gates, then keep straight on through two fields, beside a left-hand hedge at first, then later a fence, with views of a restored timber-framed cottage ahead. At the far end of the second field go straight on through a narrow chain-gate and take a hedged path to emerge at a bend in the cottage drive.

Take this drive straight on, then, where it bears left by the entrance to Gaddesden Hall, turn right through a hedge gap (still on path GG57) and cross a stile. Now turn left over a stile by a gate and follow left-hand fences through two paddocks and a large field with close-up views of the partly sixteenth-century, part-flint and part-brick Gaddesden Hall to your left at first, then passing a fish farm to your left. At the far end of the large field go straight on over a stile, then take fenced path HH12 round the edge of a field, eventually passing through a kissing-gate. Now continue along a fenced path round a water pumping station to emerge through a second kissing-gate onto a macadam drive (byway HH13). Turn left onto this drive to reach the A4146, then cross the main road carefully and take byway HH13 straight on, crossing a bridge over the River Gade to reach Piccott's End's main street. Turn right onto this and follow it for over a quarter mile, passing the fine timber-framed Piccott's End Farm to your right and eventually reaching your starting point.

WALK 20   Flamstead

Length of Walk: 5.5 miles / 8.9 Km
Starting Point: Entrance to Flamstead Recreation Ground.
Grid Ref: TL077147
Maps: OS Landranger Sheet 166
       OS Pathfinder Sheet 1095 (TL01/11)
How to get there / Parking: Flamstead, 4 miles south of
Luton, may be reached by leaving the M1 at Junction 9
and taking the A5 towards Dunstable and Whipsnade,
almost immediately turning left at the first turning sign-
posted to Flamstead. At a T-junction in the village by the
'Three Blackbirds`, turn right into Chapel Road, then take
the first turning left (Mill Lane) where you can park.
Notes: Heavy nettle growth may be encountered in places in
the summer months.

Flamstead, a corruption of 'Verlamstead`, on its hilltop above the
Ver valley, has an attractive village centre with half-timbered
and flint cottages and a row of almshouses dating from 1669, but
is dominated, when seen from afar, by its magnificent twelfth-
century church with a massive tower incorporating Roman
bricks and a small mediaeval spire known as a 'Hertfordshire
spike`. The church also boasts some of the finest mediaeval murals
in Hertfordshire, which were only rediscovered in about 1930, as
well as exquisite seventeenth- and eighteenth-century marble
monuments by Stanton and Flaxman and is the burial place of
the founder of the renowned transport firm, Thomas Pickford,
who died in 1811. Despite being less than a mile from both the
M1 and the A5, Flamstead has remained a remarkably quiet,
rural village and, with its open, hilly surroundings offers a
selection of pleasant walks with fine views.

This walk takes you from Flamstead across the Ver valley to
explore the open hills to the north. On nearing the Bedfordshire
hamlet of Pepperstock, you take a green lane southwestwards
through areas of woodland before dropping with views of the Ver
valley into Markyate. Your return route then leads you back
along the southern slopes of the Ver valley with fine views across
the valley and towards Flamstead with its prominent church.

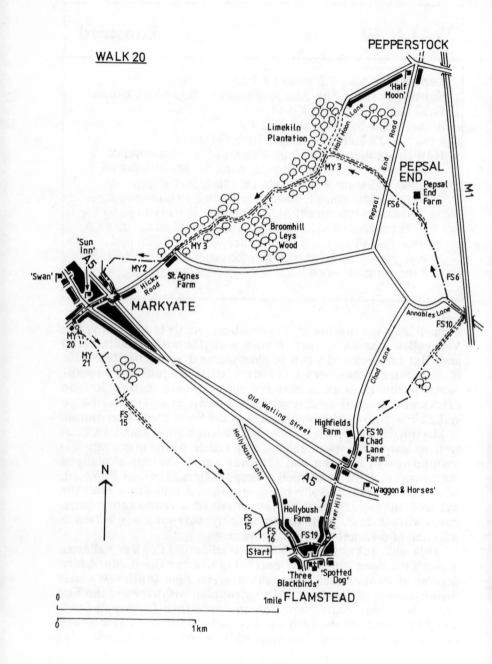

WALK 20

PEPPERSTOCK

'Half Moon'

Half Moon Lane

Limekiln Plantation

MY 3

Pepsal End Road

PEPSAL END

Pepsal End Farm

FS6

M1

Broomhill Leys Wood

Pepsal End

FS6

'Sun Inn'

A5

MY 2

MY 3

Hicks Road

St. Agnes Farm

'Swan'

MARKYATE

Annables Lane

FS10

Chad Lane

MY 20

MY 21

Old Watling Street

Highfields Farm

FS10 Chad Lane Farm

FS 15

Hollybush Lane

A5

'Waggon & Horses'

N

River Hill

Hollybush Farm

FS 15

FS 16

FS19

Start

'Three Blackbirds'

'Spotted Dog'

FLAMSTEAD

0

1mile

0

1km

Starting from the entrance to Flamstead Recreation Ground at the junction of Chapel Road, Hollybush Lane and Mill Lane, take Hollybush Lane, then immediately turn right onto fenced path FS19 between houses to a stile into a field with a view opening out across the Ver valley to your left. Now follow a right-hand hedge straight on to a stile in a corner then continue along a drive to River Hill. Turn left and take its footway downhill out of the village to cross the River Ver, then up again to the A5. Cross this fast road carefully and take a narrow lane straight on uphill to a staggered crossroads with Old Watling Street on the line of the ancient Roman road from Dover via London, Verulamium (St.Albans) and Durocobrivae (Dunstable) to Holyhead. Turn right onto this, then immediately left into Chad Lane and follow it uphill. By Chad Lane Farm turn right over a stile onto path FS10 following a right-hand hedge downhill and up again through two fields, wiggling somewhat in the second field and passing a copse before reaching a stile in the top corner of the field. Cross this stile and follow a right-hand fence straight on to the near corner of Hogtrough Wood where you join a track and follow it straight on past the wood towards the M1. Where the track starts to drop to padlocked gates, bear slightly left off it to cross a stile and descend steps into Annables Lane by its M1 underpass.

Turn left onto this road, briefly with a fine view to your left back across the Ver valley towards Flamstead. About 70 yards short of a left-hand bend turn right over a stile onto path FS6, bearing half left parallel to the M1 towards the middle of Pepsal End Farm ahead. On reaching a gate and rails, cross the rails and follow a right-hand fence straight on to a gate and rails into a fenced cattle track, which you follow beside a right-hand hedge. Where the cattle track turns right towards the farm, go straight on over rails by a gate and follow a right-hand hedge to a gate and stile onto Pepsal End Road at Pepsal End. Bear slightly right across this road and take a green lane virtually opposite straight on for a third of a mile, with fine views to your left in places across the Ver valley towards Flamstead, to reach the edge of a wood called Limekiln Plantation about a quarter mile from the Bedfordshire hamlet of Pepperstock.

Here turn left into Half Moon Lane (byway MY3), a green lane along the edge of the wood, ignoring a branching path to your left and dropping into a valley where you leave the wood. Now ignore a branching green lane to your left and take byway MY3 straight on uphill through Broomhill Leys Wood. On leaving the wood, a gap in the right-hand hedge briefly allows views towards Slip End before you pass through a copse and continue along a green lane to a bend in a road. Here take Hicks Road straight on. After 150 yards turn right over a stile onto path MY2 with a view opening out across the Ver valley at Markyate. Bear slightly right across the field, passing just left of an electricity pole to reach a hedge corner where you bear right and after about 10 yards turn left over a concealed stile. Now, walking parallel to the left-hand hedge at first, head for a stile in the hedge by a cattle trough. Cross this and take a residential road called The Ridings downhill to its junction with Hicks Road. Here cross Hicks Road and the footbridge over the A5. At the far end of the footbridge turn right down the steps and take the continuation of Hicks Road into the centre of Markyate.

Markyate, formerly Markyate Street or even Market Street, grew up as a long straggle of mainly eighteenth-century buildings along Watling Street, now High Street, which till 1897 formed the boundary between Hertfordshire and Bedfordshire. Although the village was bypassed by the modern A5 in 1957, a number of coaching inns still bear witness to the fact that the main road used to run through the village. In 1605 the sixteenth-century 'Sun Inn' was the scene of the arrest of a servant of Ambrose Rookwood, one of the conspirators in the Gunpowder Plot and it is also claimed that the highwayman, Dick Turpin once stayed here. Legend also has it that Lady Katherine Ferrers, a seventeenth-century widow from nearby Markyate Cell, became a highwayman and met a violent death and her ghost is said to haunt the house and the A5.

At a T-junction turn right into High Street, then immediately left into Pickford Road. After 150 yards by house no.21 turn left onto path MY20 along a drive into an enclosed sunken way which you follow uphill. Where the sunken way forks, go left onto path MY21 passing left of a gate then following the right-hand side of a hedge straight on. Ignore a branching path to your left, then, where the hedge ends and views open out down the Ver valley and along the ridge towards Flamstead, follow the top of a small grassy bank straight on. On reaching a crossing track, take path FS15 straight on along a grassy track, eventually passing under a sycamore tree where the track narrows to a grass crop break and continuing to a hedge. Here do **not** go through the hedge gap but turn left beside the hedge. Just before a corner, turn right over a concealed stile and follow a left-hand hedge through three fields. At the far end of the third field cross a stile and take a fenced path straight on past two more fields. Near the far side of the second field turn left over a stile onto path FS16 and head for gates and a stile left of the cream-painted Hollybush Farm. Here cross the stile and Hollybush Lane and turn right along its footway for your starting point.

WALK 21   Caddington

Length of Walk: 5.4 miles / 8.7 Km
Starting Point: Caddington Church.
Grid Ref: TL064198
Maps: OS Landranger Sheet 166
             OS Pathfinder Sheets 1072 (TL02/12) &
             1095 (TL01/11)
How to get there / Parking: Caddington, 2 miles southwest of
    Luton, may be reached by leaving the M1 at Junction 10
    (Luton South) and taking the A1081 towards Harpenden
    and St. Albans. After nearly half a mile turn right onto a
    road signposted to Slip End, Caddington and Markyate.
    At its junction with the B4540 follow it straight on towards
    Caddington and Luton, then, at a T-junction by the ´Barn
    Owl`, turn left for Caddington. In the village drive past the
    ´Chequers` and the church then turn left or right into one
    of the side-roads and find a suitable place to park.
Notes: Heavy nettle growth may be encountered in places in
    the summer months.

Caddington with its attractive village green on an upland plateau
separating the Ver and Lea valleys has suffered somewhat from
its proximity to the M1 and the expanding towns of Luton and
Dunstable, which have swamped it with a rash of modern housing
development, but green belt policies have, so far, saved it from
being swallowed up by either town and it remains a good centre
for a whole series of attractive Chiltern walks. The village, traditionally a centre of the brick- and tilemaking industry, boasts a
parish church of Saxon origin with Saxon quoins in one wall and
a Norman doorway with the characteristic zigzag decoration but
heavy restoration in 1875 obscured much of its history. Human
habitation of the area, however, goes back much further as in the
1890s the Dunstable archaeologist, Worthington Smith,
discovered in a claypit at Castle End a 250,000-year-old axe-
maker´s workshop with finished flint blades, flint flakes which had
been struck off them and a pile of unused flints.
   The walk leads you northwestwards from Caddington along
the ridge to the Chiltern escarpment at Blow´s Down with its
superb views across Luton, Dunstable, Houghton Regis and the

95

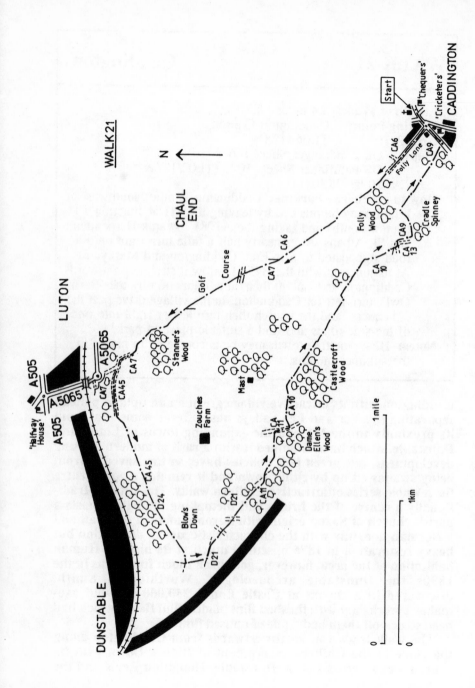

WALK 21

N

CADDINGTON

'Chequers'
'Cricketers'

Start

CA6
Folly Lane
CA9

Folly Wood
CA9
CA 13
CA 10
Cradle Spinney

CHAUL END

Golf Course
CA6
CA7

LUTON
A505
A5065
'Halfway House'
A505
A5065
CA7
CA45
CA7
Stanners Wood

Zouches Farm
Mast

Castlecroft Wood
CA 10
CA 11
Dame Ellen's Wood

CA45
D24
Blow's Down
D21
CA11
D21

DUNSTABLE

1 mile
1km

surrounding countryside before returning by a parallel route to Caddington.

Starting from Caddington Church, take the major road southwestwards past the green and Manor Road to your left, then turn right into Folly Lane (bridleway CA6) and follow it out of the village. Where the macadam road bears right into a mobile home site, take a pleasant green lane straight on to enter a field. Here take path CA6 straight on along the outside edge of Folly Wood at first, then ignoring a hedge gap to your left and following a left-hand hedge straight on. After 250 yards, just past a lightning-damaged ash tree, go straight on through a somewhat overgrown gap in a kink in the hedge and follow a sporadic right-hand hedge straight on to the far end of the field. Here go through a hedge gap onto the Vauxhall Recreation Club Golf Course and bear slightly left onto path CA7 heading for the far left-hand corner of the golf course just right of the right-hand end of Stanner's Wood, crossing a stony track and a bridge over a ditch by a wooden marker post and a further bridge over another ditch. At the far corner of the golf course go straight on through a hedge gap and follow a right-hand hedge to a corner of Stanner's Wood, where you follow the outside edge of the wood then a left-hand hedge straight on with fine views opening out to your right across Luton towards Warden Hill and Galley Hill.

On entering a green lane, continue downhill to a stile. Some 20 yards further on by a marker post, turn left onto path CA45 following a terraced grassy track beside a left-hand fence gently up onto Blow's Down with fine views opening out to your right and ahead across Luton, Dunstable and Houghton Regis. On reaching an old gateway, go through it and bear slightly left, joining a left-hand fence and sporadic hedge, which you follow for over half a mile through two fields, passing an old chalk quarry to your right and (now on path D24) entering scrubland. Eventually you emerge from the scrubland over a stile by a gate above the historic town of Dunstable at the crossroads of the prehistoric Icknield Way and Roman Watling Street, site of a twelfth-century royal lodge and magnificent priory, part of which has survived as the parish church.

Now go straight on along the ridge following a slightly sunken track and heading just left of an electricity pylon. Where the track ends at the end of the ridge, go straight on downhill towards an area of scrub in an old chalkpit. Just before reaching this, turn left onto a worn path which joins a terraced track under a powerline, keeping right at a fork and passing right of the next pylon. Now on path D21, you enter a distinct sunken way which you follow uphill ignoring two crossing tracks and eventually joining the top fence of the downland field. Where the track peters out, take a terraced path straight on to cross a stile into scrubland. Now take path CA11 straight on through the scrubland, eventually bearing left to reach a crossing path by another marker post. Here go straight on through a hedge gap into a field where a telecommunications mast comes into view ahead and you turn right and follow a right-hand hedge. By another marker post bear half left onto what is normally a grass crop break across the field to a corner of Dame Ellen´s Wood, then follow its edge straight on to reach the private road to Zouches Farm.

Turn right onto this road, then, at the far end of the left-hand field, turn left onto path CA10 following a right-hand hedge. At the far side of the field go straight on through a hedge gap then bear right into a sunken way along the edge of Castlecroft Wood, soon emerging onto a field headland and continuing through two fields to the far end of the wood. Here follow a right-hand hedge straight on under a powerline. Where the hedge bears left, go through a gap in it and bear slightly left across the next field, gradually diverging from the powerline to cross a stile in the far hedge left of the powerline and an ash tree. Now turn left and follow the left-hand hedge for 50 yards to another marker post where you bear right across the field to join a left-hand hedge by a marker post at the far end of a copse to your left. At the far side of the field go straight on over a stile to reach a bend in a green lane (bridleway CA13).

Turn left into this green lane, then take path CA9 straight on through a hedge gap into a field and immediately turn right to follow the back of the lane hedge to a field corner. Here turn left and follow the edge of Cradle Spinney uphill. At the far end of the spinney, where Caddington comes into view to your right, go through a gap and follow the right-hand side of a line of trees to a field corner. Here turn right and follow a left-hand hedge to the far end of the field, then go straight on through a hedge gap and scrubby woodland to reach a squeeze-stile onto Dunstable Road. Cross the road carefully (beware - poor visibility!), then turn left along its pavement to reach your starting point.

WALK 22   Dunstable Downs

Length of Walk: (A) 3.9 miles / 6.4 Km
(B) 1.8 miles / 3.0 Km
(C) 2.4 miles / 3.8 Km

Starting Point: Noticeboard at rear right-hand corner of main Dunstable Downs car park.

Grid Ref: TL008198

Maps: OS Landranger Sheets 165 (Walks A & C only) & 166 (all)
OS Explorer Sheet 2 (or old Pathfinder Sheet 1094 (SP81/91)) (Walks A & C only) & Pathfinder Sheets 1072 (TL02/12) (Walks A & B only) & 1095 (TL01/11) (all)

How to get there / Parking: Dunstable Downs car park, 1.5 miles south of the town centre, may be reached from it by taking the B489 towards Aston Clinton, then turning left onto the B4541 towards the Downs and Whipsnade. At the top of the hill, park in one of the right-hand car parks near a low building with a pointed roof (the Countryside Centre and toilet block).

The Dunstable Downs, with their spectacular views along the Chilterns to Ivinghoe Beacon and out over the Vale of Aylesbury towards Oxfordshire and the Cotswolds, are today a real ´honeypot` for people from Dunstable, Luton and farther afield, for picnics and walks with superb views and convenient parking. Four thousand years ago these hills must also have been frequented, as at the northern end of the Downs are the Five Knolls, five huge Neolithic or Bronze Age barrows, where excavations have not only revealed remains from this period, but also a large number of skeletons originating from the fifth century AD, some of whom had injured bones or their hands tied behind their backs suggesting that they were the victims of some battle or massacre.

All three walks explore the Downs; Walks A and B leading you northwards along the ridge with superb views passing a spectacular coombe called Pascomb Pit and the Five Knolls before descending to the edge of Dunstable. You then double back along the foot of the Downs passing the bottom of Pascomb Pit before Walk B climbs steeply back to the car park. Walk C drops

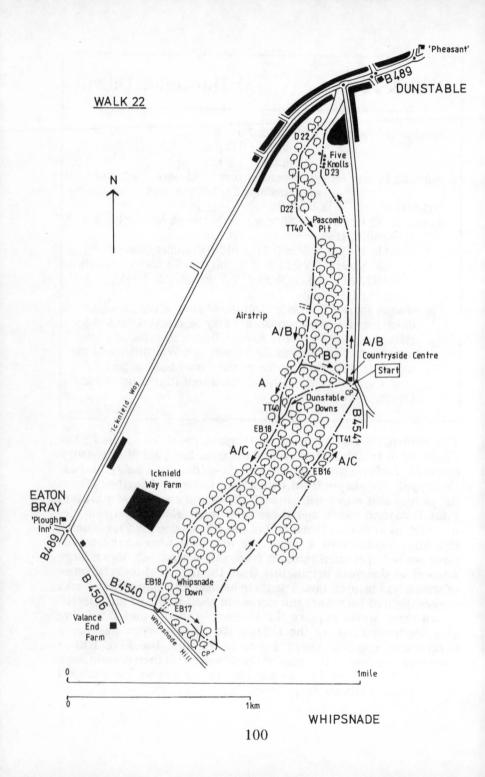

WALK 22

N

'Pheasant'

B 489

DUNSTABLE

D 22

Five
Knolls

D 23

D 22

Pascomb
Pit

TT40

Airstrip

A/B

A/B

Countryside Centre

B

Start

A

CP

TT40

C

Dunstable
Downs

EB18

B 4541

A/C

TT41

EB16

A/C

Icknield way

Icknield
Way Farm

EATON
BRAY

'Plough
Inn'

B 489

B 4506

B 4540

EB18

Whipsnade
Down

EB17

Valance
End
Farm

Whipsnade Hill

CP

0   1mile

0   1km

WHIPSNADE

100

from the car park with fine views to join **Walk A** at the foot of the Downs where both continue to the bottom of Whipsnade Downs. You then climb to the top of the Downs before returning along the ridge with superb views to reach the car park.

Walks A & B start by the noticeboard in the rear right-hand corner of the main Dunstable Downs car park and take a macadam path, ignoring a branching path to your right. Where the macadam path bears right towards the Countryside Centre, leave it and go straight on, taking a track through the centre of an overflow car park with fine views along the Downs ahead, over a glider airstrip towards Eaton Bray, Totternhoe and the Totternhoe Knolls to your left and towards Ivinghoe Beacon over your left shoulder. At the far end of the car park take the right-hand of two worn paths straight on, eventually reaching a set of gates. Go through the smaller gate then bear slightly left to join a worn path which you follow past the rim of the deep, steep-sided coombe called Pascomb Pit, with views opening out to your right across Dunstable, Luton and Houghton Regis towards Blow´s Down, Warden Hill, Galley Hill and Sundon. At a hilltop bear half right onto path D23, passing left of four of the Five Knolls, then continuing downhill through a kissing-gate.

On reaching an area of mown grass on the edge of Dunstable, turn left to reach the left-hand end of a row of sycamore trees, then turn left again onto path D22, following a right-hand hedge into scrubland, soon with an enclosing fence to your left. Take this path straight on through the scrubland, soon with views to your right towards Edlesborough with its prominent fourteenth-century church and Ivinghoe Beacon and later with views further to your right towards Eaton Bray, Totternhoe and Totternhoe Knolls and ahead towards Whipsnade Downs and the glider airstrip. On reaching a gate and kissing-gate, go through the kissing-gate and take worn path TT40 straight on across downland, following the contours of the hillside, now with wide views ahead and to your right. At a fork, keep right taking the major path downhill to the bottom of Pascomb Pit where you bear right, soon joining a right-hand fence. Now follow it for over a third of a mile, ignoring the gates of a bridleway to your right and various paths up the escarpment to your left. On reaching gates ahead, **Walk A** goes straight on through them disregarding a branching path to your left and continuing along the foot of the hill for 350 yards until you reach a waymarked path to your left where you go straight on joining Walk C. Now omit the next two paragraphs.

Just before the gates, **Walk B** turns left onto a permissive path climbing steeply beside a right-hand fence. Halfway up the hill, stop for a rest and turn round for a view across the glider airstrip towards Totternhoe, then continue uphill to gates leading to the open hilltop with the Countryside Centre and your starting point straight ahead.

Walk C starts by the noticeboard in the rear right-hand corner of the main Dunstable Downs car park and takes a macadam path downhill. Where the path forks, leave it and bear slightly left across the grass onto a waymarked chalky permissive path descending the hillside with fine views ahead across a glider airstrip towards Totternhoe and Totternhoe Knolls and soon to your right, along the Downs to Pascomb Pit and the hill above and to your left towards Edlesborough with its prominent fourteenth-century church and Ivinghoe Beacon, with the path gradually bearing left. Near the bottom of the hill at a fork go left, almost immediately joining Walk A.

Walks A & C now take path EB18 straight on through scrubland, soon bearing right and dropping to a stile where you ignore branching paths to left and right. Now continue along the bottom of the hillside for three-quarters of a mile with fine views to your right in places, eventually disregarding a branching path to your left and crossing two stiles to reach the B4540 near the foot of Whipsnade Hill. Turn left onto this road, then almost immediately left again onto sunken bridleway EB17. On reaching a padlocked gate, turn right and take a fenced bridleway steeply uphill, soon with fine views over your left shoulder towards Totternhoe and Totternhoe Knolls and later to your right towards the White Lion on the hillside below Whipsnade Zoo and Ivinghoe Beacon. Eventually the enclosing fences give way to scrubland and you ignore first a crossing bridleway, then a crossing footpath.

Near the top of Whipsnade Downs at a T-junction, turn left onto a permissive path, soon passing through a bridlegate and then following a right-hand hedge, later a fence then a plantation, along the top of the Downs, turning right then left at one point, with superb views to your left across the Vale of Aylesbury and later ahead towards Dunstable Downs. At the far end of the plantation take a worn path straight on, passing right of an electricity pylon to reach a bridlegate in the far right-hand corner of the field. Go through this and turn left along a fenced path downhill. On reaching a bridlegate in the left-hand fence, turn right onto bridleway EB16 through scrubland to emerge onto open downland, then take path TT41 straight on over a rise to reach the car park.

WALK 23   Totternhoe Knolls

Length of Walk: (A) 3.8 miles / 6.1 Km
(B) 3.6 miles / 5.9 Km

Starting Point: Entrance to Totternhoe Knolls Nature
Reserve car park.

Grid Ref: SP986217

Maps: OS Landranger Sheet 165
OS Pathfinder Sheet 1071 (SP82/92)

How to get there / Parking: Totternhoe Knolls, 2 miles west
of the centre of Dunstable, may be reached from the town
by taking the B489 towards Aston Clinton for nearly 1
mile. Near the edge of the town, turn right onto the road
signposted to Totternhoe. On reaching the village, follow
the priority road looking out for a signpost to the 'Nature
Reserve`, where you turn right up a rough macadam lane
to reach Totternhoe Knolls Nature Reserve car park.

Notes: Heavy nettle growth may be encountered on path
TT23 in the summer months.

Totternhoe Knolls and the village of Totternhoe below appear to
have been inhabited for thousands of years as, when chalk-
quarrying encroached on the nearby Iron Age hill fort called
Maiden Bower, it was discovered that this had been raised above
a Neolithic causewayed enclosure. The Romans, who built
nearby Watling Street (now the A5) and had a staging post at
Dunstable called Durocobrivae, also built a villa near Church
End; the Saxons, who gave the village its name meaning 'look-
out house hill`, appear to have used Castle Hill for defence
purposes and the Normans built a motte-and-bailey castle with
wooden fortifications on it which was known as Eglemunt Castle.
Although this castle was never rebuilt in stone, in the twelfth
century stone began to be mined from Castle Hill which was used
in building Windsor Castle and to build Totternhoe's fine
fifteenth-century church and this stone can also be seen forming
the corners and door and window frames of many predominantly
flint Chiltern churches. The village, which comprises three 'ends` -
Church End, Middle End and Lower End - also boasts a number
of attractive cottages and inns including the seventeenth-century,
thatched, timber-framed 'Cross Keys` on the route of Walk A.

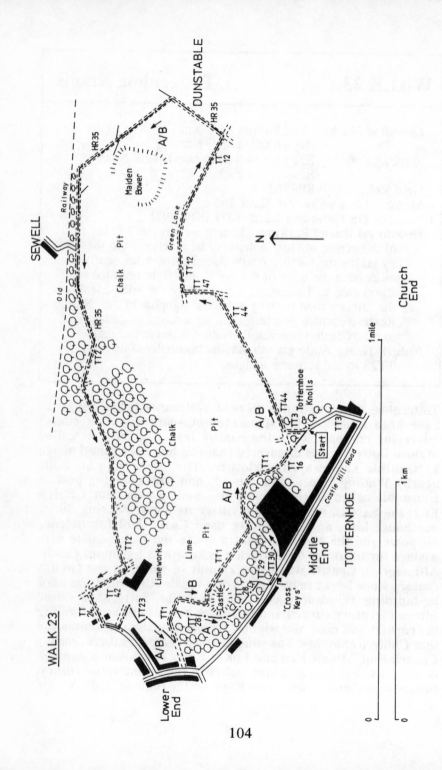

WALK 23

SEWELL

DUNSTABLE

Railway

HR 35

A/B

Maiden Bower

Chalk Pit

Old

HR 35

N ←

Green Lane

TT 12

TT 47

TT 44

Church End

1 mile

Chalk Pit

TT 7

Chalk

Pit

TT 44

A/B

Tottenhoe Knolls

TT 2

Lime works

Lime Pit

TT 1

TT 3
TT 3

Start

TT 16

A/B

TT 42

TT 24

TT 23

TT 1

A/B

TT 1

Lower End

A/B

A

28

TT 1

28

Castle

A

B

TT 29
TT 30

'Cross Keys'

Middle End

TT 3

Castle Hill Road

TOTTERNHOE

1 km

0   1 km

0   1 mile

Both walks lead you from the Nature Reserve car park to the crest of the ridge which you follow towards Dunstable with superb views towards the Downs. You then circle round passing close to Maiden Bower and the picturesque hamlet of Sewell before reaching the limeworks and climbing Castle Hill. Walk B then leads you straight back along the ridge to your starting point while Walk A passes beneath the castle mound with more fine views and drops through woodland to the ´Cross Keys` before climbing again to reach your starting point. Although the walks differ little in length, Walk A is more strenuous as it involves an additional steep climb.

Both walks start from the entrance to Totternhoe Knolls Nature Reserve car park and turn right onto bridleway TT3, the continuation of the approach road and follow it uphill to a T-junction where a fine view opens out ahead across a restored chalk quarry towards Stanbridge, Tilsworth and Toddington. Here turn right onto path TT44 taking a wide green road uphill, soon with fine views to your right towards Dunstable Downs and over your right shoulder towards Ivinghoe Beacon and Aston Hill. Continue over the hill, where the edge of Dunstable comes into view. Where the right-hand hedge ends, turn left onto byway TT47, a wide grassy track beside a left-hand hedge, soon with a second hedge to your right. Where the green road turns right, follow it (now on byway TT12) for almost another half mile over a slight rise to a crossing green road.

Turn left here onto byway HR35, a wide grassy track following a left-hand hedge a field´s length from the edge of Dunstable, with Houghton Regis´s prominent fourteenth-century church coming into view ahead. Where the hedge and track bear left, follow them, looking out for Maiden Bower, a large circular hedge-capped hill fort in the left-hand field. By Maiden Bower the track becomes enclosed by a second hedge and starts to descend to reach the fence of Sewell Cutting, part of the former Dunstable Branch of the London & North Western Railway which closed in 1962 where Roman pottery was found during construction of the railway in 1859 and which is now a nature reserve noted for its chalkland flowers. Here the lane bears left and continues downhill past a restored chalk quarry to the bottom of the hill.

Now ignore the end of Sewell village street passing between the piers of a former railway bridge to your right and take a fenced track straight on, gradually diverging from the old railway. On emerging into a field, take a grassy track straight on across it, soon entering a green lane. Now on byway TT2, follow this lane straight

105

on for two-thirds of a mile to Totternhoe Limeworks. On nearing the limeworks, ignore a crossing track, then turn right into another green lane (TT42). After 200 yards, at a junction of tracks, turn left onto bridleway TT24, a rough lane leading to the end of a macadam road at Totternhoe Lower End. Take this road straight on to the limeworks gates. Here turn left onto fenced path TT23 to the right of the gates and drive, soon turning right, then left, then right again across fields to reach a squeeze-stile leading in a few yards to a green lane (TT1). Turn sharp left onto this, following it up Castle Hill. Some 50 yards before a sharp right-hand bend, by a stile to your right, **Walk B** continues along TT1, turning sharp right and then sharp left by the castle and after a quarter mile turning sharp left again to rejoin Walk A. Now omit the next paragraph.

Walk A turns right over the stile onto path TT28 leading into an undulating area called `Little Hills` where Totternhoe stone was quarried from the twelfth century onwards and where to your left is the castle mound capped by the earthworks of the wooden Norman Eglemunt Castle superimposed on a Bronze Age fort. Here ignore a branching path to your right and bear slightly left across the undulating ground passing through a deep gully to reach a rise near the bottom of the castle mound where there are fine views out across the Ouzel valley into the Vale of Aylesbury, then bear slightly right for a stile into scrubland. Cross this and pass through the scrub into a beechwood, then bear left, ignoring a branching path to your right and following the contours of the hill until you reach a crossing path with steps (TT29). Turn right onto this, descending steeply, ignoring two branching paths to your left and eventually reaching Castle Hill Road at Totternhoe Middle End. Cross this road and turn left along its pavement. Just past the `Cross Keys`, turn left, recrossing the road and taking path TT30 uphill through the wood, following garden fences to your right at first and ignoring two branching paths to your left and one to your right. Near the top of the hill go through a squeeze-stile and turn right onto byway TT1, rejoining Walk B.

Walks A & B now follow this green road for over a quarter mile with fine views in places towards the Dunstable Downs ahead and Ivinghoe Beacon and Aston Hill to your right. Ignore the first branching path to your right. Now, on path TT16, 100 yards further on where the main track bears left, fork right onto a fenced path with fine views to your right towards Whipsnade Downs, Ivinghoe Beacon and Aston Hill, soon reaching a squeeze-stile leading to your starting point.

WALK 24   Houghton Regis (Bidwell)

Length of Walk: 4.8 miles / 7.8 Km
Starting Point: Junction of A5120 (Bedford Road) and
Roslyn Way, Houghton Regis.
Grid Ref: TL015243
Maps: OS Landranger Sheet 166
OS Pathfinder Sheet 1072 (TL02/12)
How to get there / Parking: Bidwell, 1.5 miles north of the
centre of Dunstable, may be reached from the town by
taking the A5 towards Milton Keynes and turning right
onto the A5120 towards Ampthill, which then turns left by
Houghton Regis Church. A third of a mile further on, just
before the 30 m.p.h. limit gives way to 40 m.p.h., turn left
into Roslyn Way and look for a suitable parking space,
taking care not to obstruct private driveways.
Notes: At the time of writing, paths HR14 and HR45 were
seriously obstructed, but remedial action had been
promised by South Bedfordshire DC. Should these paths
still be obstructed, an alternative route via bridleway
HR22, roads in Houghton Regis and path HR48 is
indicated on the plan. Path HR14 is also prone to heavy
nettle growth in the summer months.

Bidwell, an attractive hamlet of Houghton Regis at the foot of the
hill on the Bedford road with an inn and half-timbered farm-
houses and cottages, has today almost been swallowed up by its
larger neighbour which has expanded to a mere 100 yards from
the start of the hamlet. The mother ´village` with its fine
fourteenth-century church, large village green and some thatched
cottages must once also have been picturesque, but, since the
1960s, it has been swamped with modern housing and commercial development which have made its character suburban. The
name Houghton Regis is of Saxon origin, its first part meaning
´settlement on a hill` and its second denoting that it was a royal
manor and it was this which saved the village from being sacked
when visited by William the Conqueror soon after the Battle of
Hastings. This was also the reason for nearby Dunstable (which
then belonged to the manor) being chosen as the site for Henry
I´s palace and priory, of which Dunstable´s present magnificent

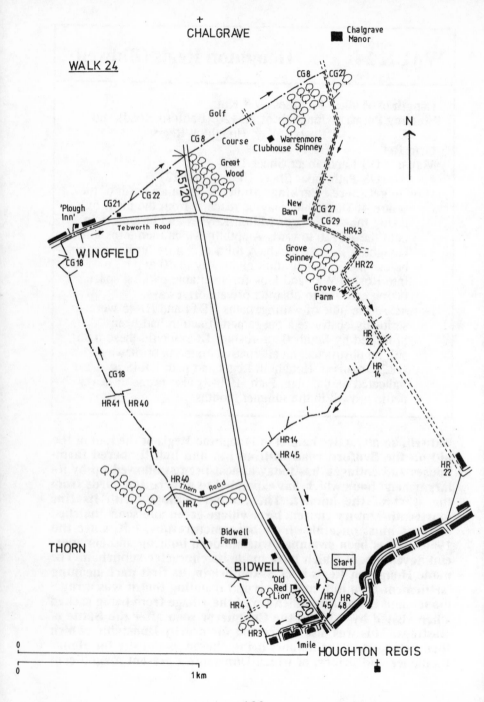

+
CHALGRAVE

Chalgrave
Manor

WALK 24

CG8   CG27

Golf

N

CG8   Course   Warrenmore
Clubhouse Spinney

A5120

Great
Wood

New   CG 27
'Plough   CG21   CG22   Barn   CG 29
Inn'   HR43
Tebworth Road

WINGFIELD   Grove
CG18   Spinney   HR22

                                      Grove
                                      Farm

CG18   HR
                                                        22

HR41   HR40   HR
                                                            14

                          HR14
                          HR45   HR
                                                                22

                    Thorn Road
HR40
            HR4

                    Bidwell
THORN   Farm

                BIDWELL
                'Old
                Red   Start
                Lion'
                        A5120   HR   HR
        HR4   45   48

            HR3

0   1 mile
                                    HOUGHTON REGIS   +
0   1 km

108

church was only a small part. In more recent times, the chalk, on which the village is built, brought it renewed prosperity as the straw-plait made from the white straw which grew on it was valuable to Luton´s straw-hat industry while the chalk itself was quarried for making cement.

This walk soon leads you out of this outpost of suburbia to explore the rolling Chiltern foothills to the north with their wide views, taking you by way of the ridgetop hamlet of Wingfield to skirt the lost village of Chalgrave before returning by a more easterly route.

Starting from the junction of the A5120 and Roslyn Way, take Roslyn Way uphill, soon bearing right into Plaiters Way (reminding us of the ancient craft once performed by village women). This road immediately bears left and where it turns left again, leave it and bear slightly right onto a macadam path passing right of the end of the houses ahead. Where this path ends, turn right onto fenced path HR3, following it downhill to a kissing-gate where you continue past thick scrub concealing a disused chalkpit. Eventually the path bears left and you emerge by a seat at the end of a concrete road. Here turn right, passing the seat, crossing the concrete road and a stile and taking path HR4, part of the Icknield Way long-distance path straight on across a field to the left-hand end of a hedge. Now bear half left with a view to your left towards Chalk Hill with its large chalk quarry, heading for a hedge gap and culvert by a junction of powerlines. Having crossed the culvert, bear slightly right across the next field, aiming for a black-and-white chevron sign indicating a bend on Thorn Road.

Cross this busy road carefully (beware of the blind bend to your right!), then cross a culvert and iron rails opposite onto path HR40, following a left-hand hedge and ditch through two fields. Where the hedge ends, take what is usually a crop-break straight on to the corner of another hedge. Here cross a footbridge and follow a left-hand hedge and ditch, soon bearing left and later passing under a large pylon. Near the far end of the field turn left over a footbridge onto path HR41 following a right-hand hedge and ditch, then almost immediately turn right over a second footbridge and take path CG18 following a left-hand hedge and ditch gently uphill with wide views opening out behind you towards Houghton Regis and to your left towards Totternhoe Knolls and the Ivinghoe Hills beyond. Where the hedge ends, go straight on uphill, passing just right of two overgrown ponds, then bear slightly right across the field, aiming midway between a large walnut tree and a lightning-damaged

109

ash tree on the skyline to reach the corner of a hedge. Here turn round for a fine view towards Houghton Regis behind you, then go through a hedge gap and follow a left-hand hedge, soon turning right then left and ignoring a branching path to your left, eventually reaching a squeeze-stile onto Tebworth Road, Wingfield.

Turn right onto this road and follow it through this hamlet of Chalgrave parish for over 300 yards, ignoring a branching path to your left and passing the thatched ´Plough Inn`, then, at a right-hand bend, fork left over a stile by a gate onto path CG21. Now bear half right across a field to pass just left of a modern house with a fine view to your left towards the hilltop village of Milton Bryan, then cross a stile in the far hedge where Toddington with its fine hilltop thirteenth-century church comes into view slightly to your left with the thirteenth-century church of the lost village of Chalgrave in a copse to the right of it. Now, leaving the Icknield Way long-distance path, take path CG22 straight on across the field towards the furthest right-hand of a line of steel electricity pylons to reach a hedge gap onto the A5120.

Cross this road and a stile by a gate opposite onto Chalgrave Manor golf course, then take path CG8 straight ahead towards a chalk quarry face and a line of pylons on the skyline at Sundon. On reaching a waymarking post, bear slightly left with wide views to your right towards Luton, passing just right of a wooden pylon to reach a waymarking post on the next rise left of the clubhouse. Here cross the clubhouse drive and keep straight on, soon passing the left-hand end of Warrenmore Spinney. Now cross a stile by a gate and follow a right-hand fence to a stile onto a farm road where Chalgrave Manor is to your left.

The manor and the church, the tower of which collapsed in a gale in 1888 and which is noted for its fine thirteenth- to fifteenth-century murals, are virtually all that remains of the ancient village of Chalgrave which is believed once to have been larger than its hamlets of Wingfield and Tebworth where most of the parishioners live today. The reasons for and circumstances of its depopulation and disappearance still remain a mystery.

Turn right onto the farm road (path CG27) passing a picturesque pond, ignoring the stile of a branching path to your left and continuing gently uphill for half a mile with wide views to your left towards Chalton and Sundon. Soon after the road becomes macadamed by New Barns, go through a gate and at a right-hand bend turn left through a gap by gates onto byway CG29, following a grassy track by a right-hand hedge. On passing under a powerline, the track enters a sunken way and becomes byway HR43, then, at a fork, turn right onto bridleway HR22, briefly entering a green lane and continuing downhill by a line of trees into a valley bottom. By a corner of a copse to your right called Grove Spinney, turn left onto a track passing Grove Farm where you ignore two crossing tracks and continue beside a powerline.

On reaching a culvert at the foot of a hill leading up to the edge of Houghton Regis, do **not** cross it but turn right and take path HR14, following a left-hand ditch, later a hedge through three fields. At the far side of the third field go straight on, crossing a concealed stile and following a left-hand hedge through a fourth field, eventually entering a short green lane. At the end of this go straight on, crossing a ditch and a fence and following a left-hand hedge through a fifth field, looking out for a concealed footbridge in the left-hand hedge. Turn left over this onto path HR45, following a right-hand hedge, then a ditch, then a fence and sporadic hedge. At the far end of the field go straight on through a hedge gap and across a narrow field, joining another right-hand hedge by an ash tree and following this hedge, later a fence through two fields. Where the fence turns right in the second field, bear half right across the field to reach the A5120 at Bidwell by a large elder bush some 70 yards short of the far right-hand corner of the field. Here turn left along the road for your starting point.

WALK 25   Sundon Hills

Length of Walk: 5.3 miles / 8.6 Km
Starting Point: Sundon Hills Country Park car park.
Grid Ref: TL047285
Maps: OS Landranger Sheet 166
             OS Pathfinder Sheets 1048 (TL03/13) & 1072
             (TL02/12)
How to get there / Parking: Sundon Hills Country Park, 5.5
    miles northwest of the centre of Luton, may be reached by
    leaving the M1 at Junction 12 (Toddington) and taking
    the A5120 towards Ampthill for half a mile, then turning
    right onto a road signposted to Harlington Station. In
    Harlington continue past the station to the village cross-
    roads then turn right onto the Sundon road and follow it
    for 2 miles. On nearing the top of a steep hill, turn left
    into the Sundon Hills Country Park car park.

Sundon Hills Country Park with its chalk downland rich in flora
and superb views towards Sharphoe Clappers and across the
Bedfordshire lowlands to the north is today a justifiably popular
destination for visitors from nearby towns, to which public access
was gained only thanks to its purchase by Bedfordshire County
Council. In the seventeenth century the surrounding countryside
was, however, the scene of critical events in the life of the non-
conformist preacher and author, John Bunyan, who was arrested
at Lower Samshill in 1660. Bunyan subsequently appeared
before the magistrate, Francis Wingate at his sixteenth-century
manor house in Harlington before being incarcerated for twelve
years in Bedford Gaol where he wrote his ´Pilgrim´s Progress`,
for which he is still famous today. Sundon´s large thirteenth-
century church with its mediæval murals and stone seats around
its walls for the elderly and infirm from before the introduction of
pews (from which the phrase ´the weak go to the wall` derives)
was also the setting of the wedding of William Foster, another of
Bunyan´s persecutors and Anne Wingate, the magistrate´s sister.
    The walk first leads you through the country park with its
superb views of Sharpenhoe Clappers and the lowlands below
before descending through woodlands to the foot of the Clappers.
You then continue below the escarpment, with fine views of the

hills for much of the time, to reach Harlington on its low hilltop before returning across the valley and up the escarpment for a further section of fine hillside views leading back to your starting point.

Starting from the entrance to Sundon Hills Country Park car park, take a permissive path, part of the Icknield Way long-distance path and Bunyan Trail, following the right-hand hedge through the car park, then pass through a wheelchair kissing-gate a few yards to your left. Now continue beside the right-hand hedge for half a mile with fine views ahead towards Sharpenhoe Clappers, a spur of chalk downland capped by a beech copse surrounded by an Iron Age camp, and to your left towards Harlington, Ampthill, Pulloxhill and Silsoe, later passing a redundant stile and eventually descending to a kissing-gate. Go through this and turn right onto a grassy track following a right-hand fence round the top of a steep-sided coombe, then uphill and bearing right to a gate and kissing-gate.

Do **NOT** go through these gates but fork right over a stile onto path SU19 following a sporadic left-hand hedge gently uphill to the far side of the field. Here turn left through a hedge gap onto path SU4 following the edge of Holt Wood to its far end. Now bear half left onto a track across the field to a corner of Fernhill Wood where you bear half left again. At the far side of the wood turn right off the track and continue to follow the edge of the wood to the far end of the field. Here turn left and follow the edge of a tree belt gently downhill until the path enters a wood and reaches a waymarked path junction. Now, leaving the Icknield Way and Bunyan Trail, take path SL15 straight on steeply downhill, soon descending some steps and continuing downhill until you reach the edge of the wood.

Here ignore a crossing path and take path HA25 straight on over a stile and beside a right-hand hedge towards Sharpenhoe Clappers. At a field corner bear left, now following the right-hand hedge towards ridge-top ribbon development at Harlington for a quarter mile to a footbridge. Cross this and a crossing bridleway and join a farm track following a right-hand hedge straight on to a culvert over a stream where there is a fine view of Sharpenhoe Clappers. Having crossed the culvert, turn left onto path SL39 beside a left-hand hedge and stream for over two-thirds of a mile. 200 yards beyond a sharp right-hand bend in the stream, turn left over a footbridge onto path HA5, bearing left, ignoring a second footbridge to your left and following a left-hand stream for a third of a mile to a hedge gap and wooden footbridge leading to Lower

East End Road. Cross this road and a culvert opposite and take path HA18 bearing half right and following a right-hand ditch and sporadic hedge to a field corner. Here cross a culvert then bear left beside a left-hand hedge. At the far end of the field turn right and follow a left-hand ditch, soon bearing left. Where the ditch bears right again, cross a footbridge and bear right across a large field, heading just right of a group of modern houses and left of an electricity pole to cross a footbridge just left of the far corner of the field. Now continue along a hedged path to reach Sundon Road, Harlington.

Turn left onto its nearside pavement then, where this pavement ends, cross the road and take path HA4 opposite, soon turning left over two stiles into a field. Go straight on across the field passing through the left-hand of two gates, then bear slightly right to cross two stiles flanking a tree belt. Now keep straight on to cross a stile by a gate in a field corner, then continue across the next field to cross a stile at the left-hand end of a hedge. Here turn right and follow the right-hand hedge for 350 yards. Where the hedge ends, bear half left across a neck of field to the end of another hedge, then follow its left side to the far side of the field. Here turn left and follow a right-hand ditch for 300 yards with fine views ahead of Sharpenhoe Clappers and the Sundon Hills.

On reaching a bridlebridge over the ditch, do **NOT** cross it but take bridleway HA21 straight on, rejoining the Icknield Way long-distance path and immediately turning right and following the ditch downhill towards a restored landfill site. In the field corner turn left and follow a right-hand ditch straight on through two fields. At the far side of the second field go left at a fork along the outside edge of a belt of scrub with fine views to your left towards Harlington. After 120 yards turn right into the scrub and ignoring a gate to your left, take bridleway SU3 gently uphill through the scrub for a quarter mile. On emerging through a bridlegate into a field, turn left onto path SU20, passing through a hedge gap where a fine view towards Harlington and Ampthill opens out to your left. Here turn right and follow a right-hand hedge uphill to a field corner, then turn left and follow a right-hand hedge for over a quarter mile with superb panoramic views across Bedfordshire to your left to reach a gate and kissing-gate onto Harlington Road where you turn right for your starting point.

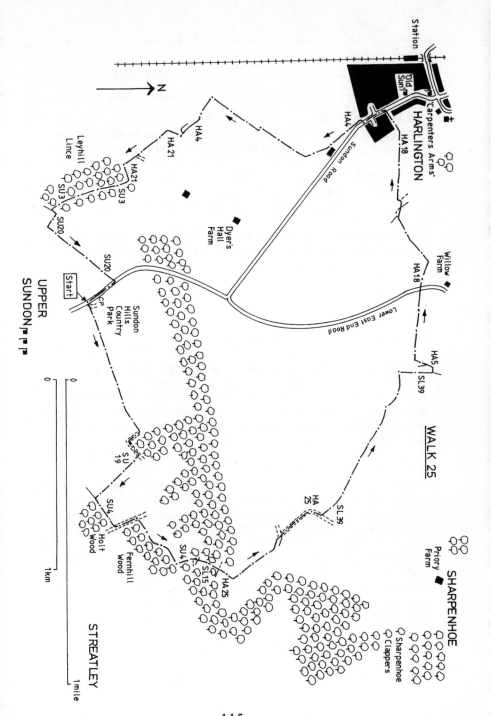

WALK 25

Station

"Carpenters Arms'
"Old Sun"
HARLINGTON

HA 18
HA4
Sundon Road

Leyhill
Lince
HA 21
HA 21
SU3
SU3
SU20

Dyer's
Hall
Farm

Willow
Farm
HA18

Lower East End Road

Start
CP
SU20

Sundon
Hills
Country
Park

HA5
SL39

UPPER
SUNDON

SU
19

SU4
Holt
Wood

Fernhill
Wood

SU4
SL15
SL15
HA25

HA
25
SL39

STREATLEY

Priory
Farm

SHARPENHOE

Sharpenhoe
Clappers

N

0

0

1km

1mile

115

WALK 26   Barton-le-Clay

Length of Walk: 2.3 miles / 3.7 Km
Starting Point: Gates of recreation ground at the junction of Old Road and Washbrook Close, Barton-le-Clay.
Grid Ref: TL083304
Maps: OS Landranger Sheet 166
OS Pathfinder Sheets 1048 (TL03/13) & 1072 (TL02/12)
How to get there / Parking: Barton-le-Clay, 6 miles north of Luton, may be reached from the town by taking the A6 towards Bedford. After about 5 miles, fork left onto the B655 towards Hitchin. On reaching the village, turn right (still on the B655), then, after 200 yards at a sharp left-hand bend, fork right into Old Road and park near its junction with Washbrook Close.

Barton-le-Clay, formerly known as Barton-in-the-Clay meaning ´barley farm in the clay land`, sits astride the old route of the A6 from London to Bedford and the Northwest of England at the foot of the Chiltern escarpment where the clay land to the north, from which its name derives, gives way to Chiltern chalk. As such, in the days of the stagecoach, Barton was a place of busy coaching inns, but earlier its history was marked by less peaceful pursuits as in 54BC the nearby Iron Age hill fort of Cassivellaunus known as Ravensburgh Castle was attacked by Julius Cæsar while the village itself was the scene of a ninth-century battle between Saxons and Danes. Despite Barton being swamped by modern housing in the 1960s and 1970s, the vicinity of its church dating from 1180 but much enlarged in the thirteenth century with its fifteenth-century tower and finely-carved roof depicting eagles, saints and apostles, its moated sixteenth-century rectory and a number of attractive cottages, remains an area of rural tranquillity and beauty. For the walker, however, Barton´s principal attraction is as a centre for walks with spectacular views of and from the range of hills which bears its name and represents the northern-most ridge in the Chilterns and it is these hills which are thought to have been the inspiration for John Bunyan´s ´delectable mountains` in his ´Pilgrim´s Progress`.

This walk, indeed, though quite short, includes some of the best of the local views, leading you towards a spectacular coombe called Windy Hollow before climbing through woodlands to the top of the escarpment. You then round the top of Windy Hollow to reach an outcrop of chalk downland with panoramic views of the surrounding countryside including Ravensburgh Castle, before descending back into Barton-le-Clay.

Starting by the recreation ground gates at the junction of Old Road and Washbrook Close, take Old Road, the original route of the London-Bedford road which was abandoned in favour of the modern A6 due to its steep ascent of the escarpment, towards the hills for a further 220 yards. Just after the road narrows, turn left through a hedge gap with a motorcycle trap onto path BC1 following a left-hand hedge to the next corner of the field. Here take a permissive path straight on through a squeeze-stile into Leet Wood and continue ahead, ignoring a branching path to your right. Having passed through another squeeze-stile, disregard a further branching path to your right and bear half left to cross a footbridge, soon reaching a field with fine views of the Barton Hills ahead and to your right.

Here turn right onto path BC15 following the outside edge of the wood. Some 100 yards short of the far end of the field by a round hill to your left known as ´Plum Pudden`, no doubt due to its shape, turn right over a footbridge, then left onto a path along the inside edge of the wood. Having passed through a kissing-gate, some 50 yards further on, fork right through another kissing-gate and bear half left onto a steep path known as The Stairway, climbing through the wood with occasional glimpses of a spectacular coombe called Windy Hollow through the trees to your left. Eventually, the path levels out and enters a clearing with fine views of the Barton Hills to your left. Now ignore a path merging from your right, then, at a T-junction of paths by a stile to your right, turn left onto path BC19, soon crossing a stile where superb views open out across the Barton Hills.

Here follow a right-hand hedge straight on, soon with additional views to your left down the coombe across Barton-le-Clay towards Pulloxhill and the Greensand Ridge beyond. At the top of a rise keep straight on, now skirting the top rim of Windy Hollow, eventually crossing a stile by a gate onto a rough track, where the left-hand end of Ravensburgh Castle, which encloses an area of no less than 22 acres, can be seen in the trees ahead. Here turn left onto bridleway BC16 following the track beside a left-hand fence past the top of Windy Hollow with views of Ravensburgh Castle in the trees to your right. Where the track forks by a stile at the corner of a fence, take bridleway BC26 straight on with superb panoramic views across Bedfordshire opening out ahead and to your right. Soon the track starts to descend and enters a sunken way which gradually bears left, eventually passing a disused chalkpit to your left where the sunken way becomes a wide green lane. On emerging into a field, turn right onto a chalky track which soon bears left and follows the edge of a right-hand tree-belt, eventually narrowing and becoming fenced. On reaching the end of Church Road with its pretty cottages, turn right along it. By the church, just before a thatched cottage, turn left onto fenced path BC4 leading to the recreation ground where you bear slightly right to reach the iron gates right of a group of birch trees at your starting point.

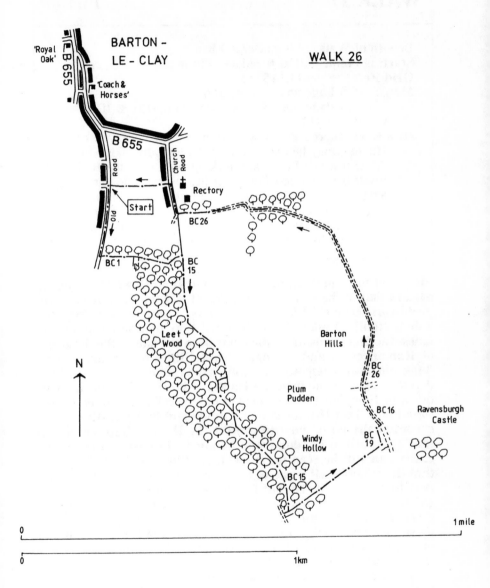

BARTON - LE - CLAY

WALK 26

'Royal Oak'

B 655

'Coach & Horses'

B 655

Old Road

Church Road

Start

Rectory

BC 26

BC 1

BC 15

Leet Wood

N

Barton Hills

BC 26

Plum Pudden

BC 16

Ravensburgh Castle

Windy Hollow

BC 19

BC 15

0   1 mile

0   1km

WALK 27   Pirton

Length of Walk: 4.9 miles / 7.9 Km
Starting Point: ´Cat & Fiddle`, Pirton.
Grid Ref: TL145315
Maps: OS Landranger Sheet 166
            OS Pathfinder Sheets 1048 (TL03/13) & 1072
            (TL02/12)
How to get there / Parking: Pirton, 3 miles northwest of
    Hitchin, may be reached from the town by taking the
    A505 towards Luton and forking right onto the B655
    towards Barton-le-Clay. After just over 1 mile, turn right
    again onto a road signposted to Pirton and Shillington.
    On entering Pirton village, ignore the first turning right,
    then take the second (Great Green) to reach a village
    green and look for a suitable parking place.

Pirton, at the foot of Knocking Hoe and High Down at the northeastern end of the Chiltern escarpment less than a mile from the
prehistoric Icknield Way, appears to be a settlement of considerable antiquity. Linked to the Icknield Way by a series of ancient
lanes, the Hertfordshire village has been the site of the discovery
of Roman coins and the name Toot Hill, a Saxon name for a
´look-out post`, suggests that the Saxons used it as part of their
defences against the bellicose Danes. Following the Norman con-
quest in 1066, however, a Norman knight called Ralph de Limesi
soon made Toot Hill the site of a motte and bailey castle with an
exceptionally large moat to protect the Hitchin Gap, an important approach to London from the north. The earthworks of this
castle can still be seen today, while further earthworks suggest
that the village itself was also fortified. From this period too is the
twelfth-century church, but following the collapse of its tower in
1874, a new tower had to be constructed in 1876 which was
given a characteristic ´Hertfordshire spike`. Today, apart from
these mediæval relics, the village can also boast a large number
of picturesque sixteenth- and seventeenth-century farms and
cottages which make it well worth a visit.
     The walk, which is very easy in nature, first leads you across
fields with panoramic views across the surrounding countryside
and of the Chiltern escarpment, to reach the Icknield Way at

West Mill near the edge of Hitchin and Ickleford. You then follow this ancient green road southwestwards, gently climbing to the top of High Down, from which you descend with fine views of High Down House and across the Bedfordshire plain, to return to Pirton.

Starting with your back to the ´Cat & Fiddle`, bear half right across the village green into Bury End and follow this cul-de-sac lane to its end. Here bear left through a kissing-gate onto path PI18, heading for a kissing-gate by a white cottage and garage, passing Toot Hill with its Norman motte and bailey castle and the parish church to your left. On emerging through the kissing-gate into Walnut Tree Road, turn right along it for 100 yards. Just past house no.11a turn left through a small iron gate onto fenced path PI5. Where its left-hand fence ends, continue to follow its right-hand fence past allotments to reach the cricket club car park. Here bear half left through the car park then continue between a left-hand fence and a line of chestnut trees past the cricket field to a squeeze-stile where you enter a large open field with superb panoramic views over the surrounding countryside.

Now bear slightly right along what is normally a grass cropbreak aiming for the near end of a hedge ahead. On reaching this hedge, follow its right-hand side straight on for three-quarters of a mile through two large fields. At the far end of the second field, go through a hedge gap into a green lane called Mill Way (bridleway PI6) where you turn right and continue along it (later on bridleway IC19) to reach the Icknield Way by Westmill Farm on the edge of Ickleford, the name of which derives from the village being the site of a ford where the Icknield Way crossed the River Hiz.

Turn right onto this ancient road, named after the Iceni, the East Anglian Belgic tribe ruled by Queen Boadicea, at the point where its macadam surface. Ignoring two sets of gates to your left and a gate to your right, go straight on through a black iron gate into a wide green lane and follow it straight on for 1 mile, eventually climbing to reach Hitchin Road at Punch´s Cross where there are fine views behind you across Hitchin. Cross this road and go straight on through a gate, then continue to follow the Icknield Way, now a grassy track beside a left-hand hedge, through two fields with fine views to your right towards Pirton and Stondon. At the far end of the second field cross a macadam drive and continue along a green lane to reach the B655 by cottages dated 1849.

Cross this fast road carefully and turn right onto its far verge, the edge of which is generally walkable. On reaching the far end of a small layby, cross back to the other side of the road and walk facing the oncoming traffic to a left-hand bend where you turn right through a hedge gap onto path PI7 following the right-hand side of a sporadic hedge downhill and up again to a stile near the top of the High Down ridge. Now bear slightly right across a down-land field to a pair of tall trees well left of High Down House. This stone house, unusual for this part of the country with its twisted chimney stacks and mullioned windows, was built in 1612 by Thomas Docwra (pronounced 'Dockray`), a descendant of Sir Thomas Docwra, Lord Grand Prior in England of the Knights of St. John in Jerusalem, in an imposing position previously occupied by an earlier house.

By the tall trees, ignore a private stile and follow a left-hand fence downhill to a stile in the bottom corner of the field. Cross this and turn right, then immediately left onto a grassy track downhill along the rear side of the hedge. By the bottom end of the hedge bear half left onto path PI22 following a grassy track across the field to reach a green lane known as Wood Lane. Here do **NOT** enter the green lane but turn right onto path PI24 following a left-hand hedge to reach Hitchin Road at Pirton. Now cross this road and take Great Green straight on back to your starting point.

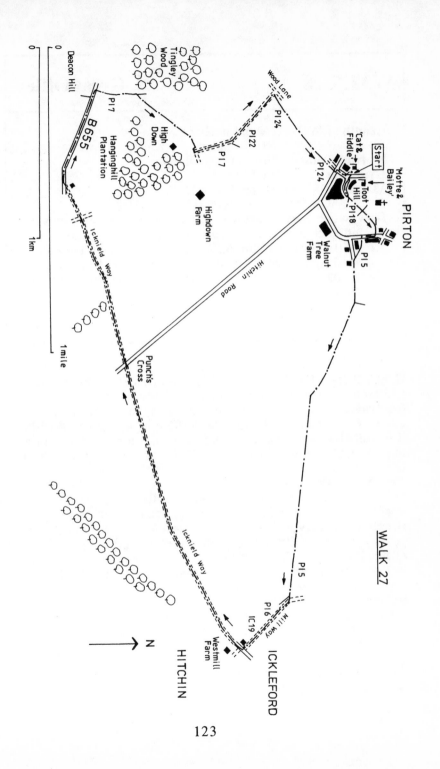

WALK 27

PIRTON

'Cat & Fiddle'

Start

'Motte & Bailey'

'Toot' Hill

Pl18

Pl15

Walnut Tree Farm

Wood Lane

Pl24

Pl24

Pl22

Pl17

Pl17

Tingley Wood

High Down

Hanginghill Plantation

Highdown Farm

Deacon Hill

B655

Hitchin Road

Icknield Way

Punch's Cross

Icknield Way

Pl5

Mill Way

Pl6

IC19

Westmill Farm

ICKLEFORD

HITCHIN

N

0

0

1km

1mile

123

WALK 28   Great Offley

Length of Walk: (A) 5.4 miles / 8.8 Km
                      (B) 4.4 miles / 7.2 Km
Starting Point: 'Bull`, Great Offley.
Grid Ref: TL143270
Maps: OS Landranger Sheet 166
            OS Pathfinder Sheet 1072 (TL02/12)
How to get there / Parking: Great Offley, 3 miles southwest
   of Hitchin, may be reached from the town by taking the
   A505 towards Luton for 2 miles, then forking left onto a
   road signposted to Great Offley, Lilley and Kings Walden.
   At the village crossroads, turn left into the High Street and
   find a suitable parking space, but do **not** use the pub car
   parks without the landlord´s permission.

Great Offley, on the old Hitchin-Luton road at the top of the Chiltern escarpment, was formerly an important stopping point for travellers whose horses or legs were weary from the steep climb. Even today, although the A505 now bypasses the village, it is still characterised by its old coaching inns. Its location also makes it an ideal centre for walking as not only does Great Offley give access to the escarpment with its steep slopes and spectacular views, but, in addition, it offers walks in the quiet and beautiful Chiltern uplands around Lilley Bottom and Kings Walden. It is therefore hardly surprising that two leading twentieth-century walkers, Don Gresswell MBE, for more than 50 years active in walking and path protection groups and founder of the Chiltern Society´s Rights of Way Group, and Ron Pigram, well-known author of London Transport and other walks books, chose to live here. The village also has a long history being named after King Offa II of Mercia, who is believed to have had a palace here and died here in 796. In the eighteenth century it was home to Sir Thomas Salusbury, Judge of the High Court of Admiralty, who rebuilt his home of Offley Place and the chancel of the thirteenth-century parish church with its beautiful fourteenth-century font and eighteenth-century monuments by Sir Robert Taylor and Nollekens.

Both walks lead you past Offley Place and the church to the edge of the village where you head east, soon with fine views towards Hitchin before descending Chalk Hill to the foot of the escarpment near Temple End where you turn north. Walk B now takes a direct route to Offley Bottom, while Walk A takes a longer route via Windmill Lane and the edge of Hitchin, both with fine views over the surrounding countryside, before both walks return by way of Offley Grange and a pleasant sylvan coombe to Great Offley.

Both walks start outside the 'Bull' in Great Offley and cross the road then turn right along its far pavement and follow it for a third of a mile past Offley Place and the church to the 'Red Lion' at the far end of the village. Here fork left into Harris Lane, an unmade road with a sign 'Unsuitable for Motors' and follow it between hedges, soon bearing right. Soon after the left-hand hedge ends, where the track forks and views open out ahead towards Hitchin, keep left and follow this track known as Chalk Hill for one and a quarter miles, ignoring all branching tracks and soon entering a green lane which descends gradually and narrows. Eventually the left-hand hedge ends and you continue beside the right-hand hedge then, on nearing Temple End, by the far end of the left-hand field and a tall ash-tree to your left, turn left into a crossing green lane called Hoar's Lane (byway H28) passing an old gate and continuing between low hedges with views of the Chiltern escarpment to your left to reach the far end of the left-hand field.

Here **Walk B** continues straight on over a rise, later with fine views to your right towards Hitchin and Stevenage. On reaching the A505 at Offley Cross, cross this fast dual-carriageway carefully and take Carter's Lane known as Wibbly-Wobbly Lane straight on for a third of a mile to a farm to your left in Offley Bottom where you turn left onto bridleway OF40 rejoining Walk A. Now omit the next two paragraphs.

Walk A turns right onto bridleway H33, crossing a field to the corner of a hedge, then following a right-hand hedge straight on with views ahead towards Hitchin Hill and Stevenage to enter a green lane known as Windmill Lane. Some 350 yards along this lane turn left through a hedge gap onto signposted path H31 bearing slightly left across a field to a hedge gap by a small elm-tree with fine views across Hitchin to your right. At the far side of the field do **not** go through the hedge gap but turn right and follow a left-hand hedge then the field boundary to another small elm-tree. Here turn left and follow a field boundary downhill, passing left of a clump of trees then following a right-hand hedge down to wooden rails onto the A505 on the edge of Hitchin.

Cross this road carefully then turn right onto its far verge. Just before the junction with Willow Lane, turn left over a stile by a gate onto path H29 following a grassy track which narrows to a crop break, later joining a sporadic left-hand hedge. At the far end of the field turn right then immediately left through a hedge gap and follow a left-hand hedge, later a crop break, straight on to the corner of a hedge on a slight rise. Keep left of this hedge and take a grassy track to reach a crossing track at a row of ash trees. Turn left onto this track, joining path H27, to reach Carter's Lane known as Wibbly-Wobbly Lane. Turn right onto this road then immediately left onto bridleway OF40, rejoining Walk B.

Walks A and B now take bridleway OF40 along a farm road passing left of Offley Bottom Farm. At the far end of the buildings, where the stone track turns right, leave it and follow a field boundary straight on, soon beneath a powerline, to reach the corner of a hedge. Now follow a sporadic left-hand hedge straight on, soon entering a green lane which climbs gently at first then drops again to reach Offley Grange. At the farm keep straight on, ignoring a crossing farm road. Where the main track turns left into a private garden, leave it and take a green lane straight on to a stile onto the A505.

Cross this fast dual-carriageway carefully by way of a staggered gap in the central reservation crash-barrier, then turn right along its far footway. Where the footway ends, turn left over a stile and take a rough drive to the old main road (beware of fast traffic approaching from your left!) Cross this road carefully and take path OF15 crossing a stile by a gate opposite and following a grassy track through woodland. On reaching a clearing, bear half right to a stile by the remains of a large fallen tree, then follow the outside edge of the wood uphill, later with a fine view towards Hitchin over your right shoulder. At the top corner of the field cross a stile and continue through woodland. Having crossed another stile, follow the outside edge of the wood straight on through two paddocks, then bear slightly right across the last paddock to a stile left of a small greenhouse. Now continue along a fenced path to reach Great Offley High Street near your starting point.

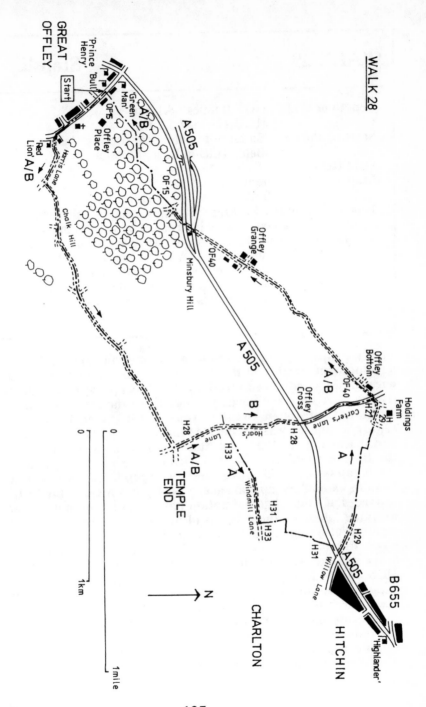

WALK 28

GREAT OFFLEY

'Prince Henry'
'Bull'
Start
Green Man'
A/B
OF5
Offley Place
Red Lion' A/B
Harris Lane
Chalk Hill
OF15
A505
OF40
Offley Grange
Minsbury Hill
A505
OF40
Offley Bottom
Holdings Farm
H
Offley Cross
A/B
Carter's Lane
H29
H27
A
B
Hoars Lane
H28
Hoo's Lane
H28
A/B
TEMPLE END
H33
A
Windmill Lane
H31
H33
H31
Willow Lane
H29
A505
B655
HITCHIN
'Highlander'
CHARLTON

0   1km
0   1mile

→ N

127

WALK 29   Stopsley

Length of Walk: (A) 5.0 miles / 8.1 Km
                    (B) 3.2 miles / 5.2 Km
Starting Point: Entrance to public car park by Barclays
                    Bank, Hitchin Road, Stopsley.
Grid Ref: TL104238
Maps: OS Landranger Sheet 166
          OS Pathfinder Sheet 1072 (TL02/12)
How to get there / Parking: Stopsley, nearly 2 miles north of
    Luton town centre, may be reached by leaving the M1 at
    Junction 10 and taking the A1081 towards Luton, then
    the A505 towards Hitchin. After a roundabout where the
    A6 is signposted to your left and you turn right, ignore
    the first turning for Stopsley, then at the next roundabout
    turn left into Stopsley where there is a signposted car park
    to your left after 90 yards.

Today Stopsley with its modern commercial and residential
development straddling the A505 has a very suburban appearance hardly conducive to walking, but this appearance is decep-
tive as after only 250 yards you can leave the town behind and
strike out into open country. Indeed, till the early twentieth
century, Stopsley was a separate village on a hilltop above Luton
and it was not till 1933 that Stopsley became incorporated into
the Borough and even in 1951 Ordnance Survey maps show a
small gap between the village and the expanding industrial town.
Despite its modern appearance, Stopsley has a very long history
as traces of Stone Age habitation have been found and its name
meaning 'glade on the ridge' is of Saxon origin. From the seventeenth century onwards, the high-quality straw which grew on its
chalk uplands also became valuable for use in the burgeoning
straw hat industry in Luton and with the coming of the railway in
1858, this industry expanded still further, while the heavy clay
capping its hilltop made Stopsley a centre for brickmaking where
the local 'Luton Greys' were produced. Despite the twentieth-
century decline of the hat industry and closure of the brickworks,
the industrial expansion of Luton has ensured that Stopsley has
remained prosperous while the high scenic value of its common
and Warden and Galley Hill to the north have so far ensured the

preservation of a 'green lung' between the pincer-like urban expansion along the A6 and A505.

Both walks first lead you across Stopsley Common with its fine views before dropping to skirt the northern suburbs of the town. Walk B then leads you up a pleasant coombe, while Walk A circles to cross the top of Warden Hill with its spectacular views, before both walks return by way of the quiet ridgetop hamlet of Butterfield Green to the suburban bustle of Stopsley.

Both walks start from the entrance to the public car park by Barclays Bank and cross Hitchin Road, then take Venetia Road virtually opposite. At its far end turn right into Lothair Road, then just past house no.37a, turn left into a macadam alleyway with safety barriers to reach playing fields on Stopsley Common. Here take path LU23 straight on along the left-hand side of a hedge. At the far end of the hedge by a single hawthorn tree turn left across the playing field, heading for the left-hand end of the third clump of trees right of a telecommunications mast on the skyline, with wide views across Luton opening out ahead. At the far side of the playing field take a worn path downhill through rough grass and a hedge gap into scrubland. Just inside the scrubland, by the frame of an old kissing-gate, turn right down several steps then fork left and continue steeply downhill to a gap by a broken kissing-gate into a field. Now bear slightly right heading for the corner of a garden wall at the right-hand end of a housing estate. Here join a gravel path and follow it to a road, onto which you turn right.

After 20 yards turn right again onto hedged path LU22. Where its left-hand hedge ends, keep following the right-hand hedge, crossing a stile at one point and continuing to the far end of a disused field. Now cross a small ditch and take path SL30 straight on with a fine view opening out towards Warden Hill ahead, joining bridleway SL29 by a marker post and continuing to the far side of the field. Here **Walk B** takes bridleway SL29 straight on along a gravel track beside a right-hand hedge for over half a mile to a crossways at the top of a ridge. Here turn right onto bridleway SL31 rejoining Walk A. Now omit the next two paragraphs.

At the far side of the field **Walk A** turns left onto bridleway SL25, a rough track beside a right-hand hedge with wide views across Luton at first, later enclosed by the fence of a housing estate. Where the right-hand hedge ends by the end of an estate road, follow a left-hand hedge straight on with views of Warden Hill to your right. On passing through a hedge gap into open grassland, bear slightly right along a worn path, ignoring crossing paths, then, where the worn path forks, go left to reach a gap in a left-hand hedge with an Icknield Way signpost. Here turn sharp right onto the first of two paths to your right (path SL26, part of the Icknield Way long-distance path), ignoring two crossing paths and continuing to a gate and kissing-gate leading to Warden Hill. Go through the kissing-gate and bear slightly right into scrubland. After about 150 yards turn left onto waymarked path SL28 (still on the Icknield Way) climbing steeply and keeping left of a large clump of hawthorn bushes to reach the top of Warden Hill where there are superb views across Luton and the surrounding countryside.

Here keep straight on along the ridge to the corner of a fence then continue along the ridgetop beside a right-hand fence. At the end of the fence go through a kissing-gate and keep straight on for 80 yards with Galley Hill (believed to be a corruption of 'Gallows Hill` as the remains of fifteenth-century gallows victims were found with fourth-century and neolithic corpses in one of the ancient barrows scattered across the hill) coming into view ahead. By a marker post leave the Icknield Way long-distance path and take a worn permissive path bearing slightly right down the hill to a kissing-gate onto bridleway SL27. (NB Should the permissive path be closed for any reason, an alternative route via public rights of way is shown on the plan). Turn right onto this bridleway following a left-hand fence. Where the fence turns left, take a grassy track straight on over a rise to the corner of a hedge. Here turn right onto bridleway SL31, a rough track following a left-hand hedge. After a third of a mile, at the far end of the right-hand field, ignore a branching path to your right and bear slightly left, now with a hedge to your right and wide views to right and left. On reaching a crossways, take bridleway SL31 straight on, rejoining Walk B.

Walks A and B now take bridleway SL31 straight on along a rough road with wide views to your right across Luton, eventually reaching the end of Butterfield Green Road by the entrance to Whitehill Farm. Take this road straight on for a third of a mile to a road junction at Butterfield Green where you bear half right across the green onto path LU25 crossing a stile by gates. Now bear left across a field heading midway between two oak trees right of Manor Farm to cross a stile into a playing field, then bear left and follow a left-hand fence. Where the fence turns left, leave it and bear slightly right across the playing field, heading just left of a tall office building at Stopsley to reach an alleyway between houses leading to the A505. Turn right onto its pavement, then, at the roundabout, turn right again for your starting point.

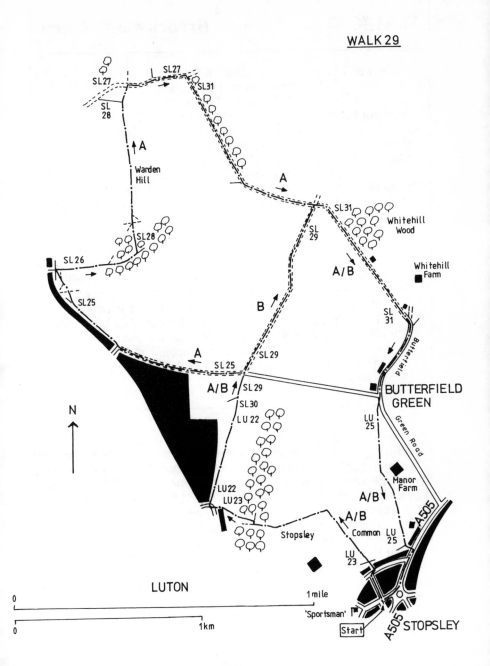

Galley
Hill

SL27
SL27
SL31
SL
28

↑A

Warden
Hill

A

SL28

SL26
SL25

SL31
Whitehill
Wood

SL
29

Whitehill
Farm

A/B

SL
31

N
↑

B

A

SL25   SL29

A/B ↑ SL29

SL30

LU 22

Butterfield Green

BUTTERFIELD
GREEN

LU
25

Green Road

LU22
LU23

A/B

A/B

Manor
Farm

A/B

Stopsley   Common   LU
25

LU
23

A505

LUTON

0 _____ 1 mile

0 _____ 1km

'Sportsman'

Start

A505   STOPSLEY

131

WALK 30   Breachwood Green

Length of Walk: (A) 5.1 miles / 8.2 Km
                        (B) 4.2 miles / 6.8 Km
                        (C) 2.5 miles / 4.0 Km

Starting Point: Junction of Oxford Road, Lower Road &
Pasture Lane, Breachwood Green.

Grid Ref: TL153220

Maps: OS Landranger Sheet 166
OS Pathfinder Sheet 1072 (TL02/12)

How to get there / Parking: Breachwood Green, 3.5 miles
east of the centre of Luton, may be reached by leaving the
M1 at Junction 10 and taking the A1081 towards Luton,
then the A505 towards Hitchin to Eaton Green Road
Roundabout, then turning right into Eaton Green Road
signposted to Tea Green. At the next roundabout bear left
then at a further roundabout turn right. Now go straight
on, soon leaving Luton behind. At a fork keep right and
follow the priority road for 1.5 miles to Breachwood
Green. In the centre of the village by the ´Red Lion`, turn
left into Oxford Road and park at its far end.

Notes: Heavy nettle growth may be encountered on Walks A
and B, particularly on bridleway PW17 in the summer
months.

Breachwood Green, a hamlet of King´s Walden parish on a
ridgetop above Lilley Bottom, would seem a very remote location
when approached through the maze of lanes between Luton and
Stevenage and indeed the history and appearance of the surrounding countryside would tend to confirm this, but it will not be long
after leaving your car before you realise that the village is
beneath the flightpath of the approach to Luton Airport. Despite
this, however, Breachwood Green, whose name derives from the
Ancient British chief Breah and whose Edwardian baptist church
can boast a pulpit used by the non-conformist preacher and
author, John Bunyan at nearby Bendish in 1658, makes a good
centre for exploring the rolling hills around Lilley Bottom which
is reminiscent of Hampden Bottom in the Chiltern heartlands but
far less well-known.

Walks A and B offer a characteristic Chiltern mixture of woodland and fine views, leading you first across Lilley Bottom to the mother village of King's Walden before passing through King's Walden Park and recrossing Lilley Bottom to reach Bendish, the scene of Bunyan's sermons. Walk B then returns by a direct route to Breachwood Green, while Walk C leads you from Breachwood Green straight to Bendish to join Walk A and both take you into another remote Chiltern 'bottom' appropriately known as Whiteway Bottom before returning to your starting point.

Walks A and B start at the junction of Oxford Road, Lower Road and Pasture Lane at Breachwood Green with its triangular island of grass and take Lower Road northeastwards then turn left into Orchard Way. On reaching a field to your right, turn right over a stile onto path KW17 bearing slightly left and following a left-hand fence downhill to cross a stile. Now turn left and follow a left-hand hedge bearing right then left. Some 50 yards beyond the corner of the hedge, by the corner of a chestnut-paling fence in the hedge, turn right onto path KW15, going straight across the field for about 100 yards to reach what is normally a crop-break. Turn right onto this joining path KW14 and follow it to a hedge gap into Watkin's Wood. Go straight on downhill through the wood and at its far side ignore a branching path to your right and keep straight on downhill beside the edge of the wood, then a left-hand hedge with fine views of Lilley Bottom, to reach the road in the valley bottom.

Cross this road and a stile opposite and passing just right of a cattle trough, go straight on uphill heading for the left-hand end of a belt of trees on the skyline to reach a stile onto fenced path KW19. Turn left onto this, soon passing through Garden Wood where you ignore branching tracks to left and right. At the far side of the wood cross a stile and bear half right, following the outside edge of the wood to a tall oak tree, then bear slightly left across a parkland field noticing a haha to the right of King's Walden Bury which is hidden in the trees, eventually reaching a gate leading to a bend in Church Road at King's Walden.

The name King's Walden is derived from the village having been a royal manor in a wooded area. Its thirteenth-century church with its notable fourteenth-century painted screen and a tower from the same period contains memorials to the Hale family who lived at the Bury from 1595 to 1885. The house bearing this name today, however, is not that of the Hales as their Elizabethan house was demolished and rebuilt in 1889, only for the same thing to happen again in 1972 when the present neo-Georgian house was built.

Now take Church Road straight on uphill, passing the church to your right and a path to Ley Green to your left, then 50 yards further on, turn right through a series of gates onto path KW23, bearing slightly left across another parkland field, with a fine view to your right at one point of the modern King´s Walden Bury, to reach a stile leading to a tree-lined drive. Cross this drive and go straight on through a kissing-gate, then follow a left-hand fence through parkland for a quarter mile ignoring the kissing-gate of a branching path. On reaching a junction of tracks by iron gates, bear slightly left, now on a stony track which continues to follow the left-hand fence for a further third of a mile to lodge gates leading to a road junction by a duckpond at Frogmore.

Here turn right onto the road passing right of the pond and follow it for half a mile, climbing at first, then descending to a T-junction in Lilley Bottom. Now turn left onto the priority road then after 130 yards turn right onto a road signposted to Bendish and follow it gently uphill for 250 yards. At a slight right-hand bend turn left through a hedge gap onto bridleway PW17 taking a grassy track beside a right-hand fence. Where the track and fence turn right, follow them, then, at a field corner, go straight on through a bridlegate and continue uphill between a fence and a sporadic hedge. At the top corner of the field turn round for a fine view across Lilley Bottom, then go straight on along a narrow green lane ignoring a gate to your right and a branching path to your left and continuing (now on bridleway PW18) to the end of a road by the entrance to West End Farm at Bendish. Turn left onto this road and follow it to a crossroads at the village green. Here go straight on, then at a further junction by a telephone box bear right. Now at a right-hand bend fork left into Long Lane, passing between a weeping willow and a sweet chestnut to reach the end of a stable block where **Walk A** leaves the road and bears half right onto path PW22 joining Walk C. Now omit the next two paragraphs.

By the end of the stable block **Walk B** turns right onto path PW24 following a power line across the field, with a view of Luton Airport ahead, to reach a hedge gap. Here bear half right and follow a right-hand hedge to reach a road onto which you turn left. Now turn immediately right onto path KW20 following a right-hand hedge. Where this hedge turns right, leave it and bear slightly left along what is normally a crop-break, passing the right-hand end of Greathouse Wood and continuing to the left-hand end of the nearer row of houses at Breachwood Green. Here join a right-hand fence and follow it to a stile leading to your starting point.

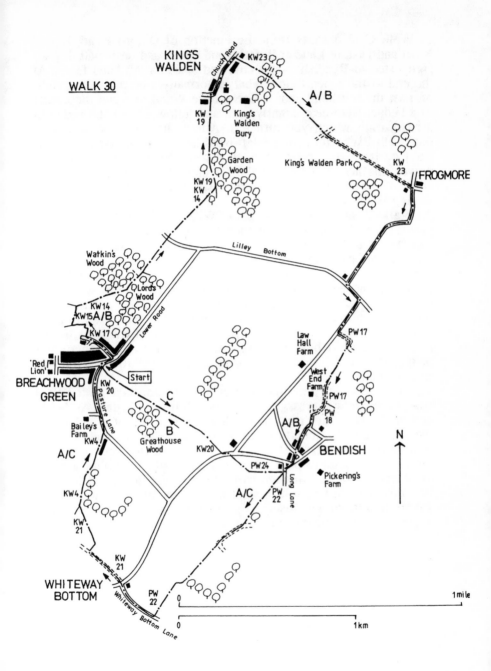

WALK 30

KING'S WALDEN

KW23

A/B

KW 19

King's Walden Bury

Garden Wood

King's Walden Park

KW 23

FROGMORE

KW 19
KW 14

Lilley Bottom

Watkin's Wood

Lord's Wood

Lower Road

Law Hall Farm

PW17

KW14
KW15 A/B

KW 17

West End Farm

PW17

'Red Lion'

BREACHWOOD GREEN

Start

KW 20

PW 18

Pasture Lane

C

A/B

Bailey's Farm

B

KW4

Greathouse Wood

KW20

BENDISH

A/C

PW24

Pickering's Farm

N

KW4

Long Lane

A/C

PW 22

KW 21

KW 21

WHITEWAY BOTTOM

Whiteway Bottom Lane

PW 22

0   1 mile

0   1 km

Walk C also starts from the junction of Oxford Road, Lower Road and Pasture Lane at Breachwood Green and takes path KW20 signposted to Bendish over a stile and beside a left-hand fence. At the end of the fence follow what is normally a crop-break straight on past the left-hand end of Greathouse Wood to reach the corner of a hedge. Here bear slightly right and follow a left-hand hedge to a road, onto which you turn left. Almost immediately turn right onto path PW24 following a left-hand hedge. At the far end of the field go through a hedge gap, then bear slightly left following a power line across a field to the far end of a stable block on the edge of Bendish where you turn sharp right onto path PW22 joining Walk A.

Walks A and C now take path PW22 crossing the field diagonally with a view of Luton Airport to your right, passing left of a single oak tree to reach a gap in the far hedge. Go straight on through this gap and across the next field to the right-hand end of a clump of trees sheltering a wartime ´pillbox` anti-aircraft gun emplacement. Here turn right onto a grassy track, then, where this track bears left, leave it and take what is normally a grass crop-break straight on with wide views ahead across Whiteway Bottom, heading towards a water-tower in trees on the skyline. At the far side of the field bear half right through the right-hand of two hedge gaps and follow a left-hand hedge downhill to Whiteway Bottom Lane.

Turn right onto this road and at a T-junction take path KW21 straight on along a grassy track beside a left-hand hedge. At the far end of the field turn right and follow the nearside of a hedge into the valley bottom, then turn left through a hedge gap and bear half right across the next field to a hedge gap in the top corner. Go through this, joining path KW4 and turn right following a right-hand tree-belt uphill through two fields. At the far end of the tree-belt bear half left to join a right-hand fence and follow it past a garage to a hedge gap leading into Pasture Lane, which you follow straight on for a quarter mile to your starting point.

INDEX OF PLACE NAMES

	Walks		Walks
Abbot's Langley	2	Dancers End	12
Aldbury	15	Deacon Hill	27
Aldbury Common	15	Drayton Beauchamp	13
Apsley	3	Dunstable	21/22/23
Asheridge	6	Dunstable Downs	22
Ashridge	17		
Askett	10	Five Knolls	22
Aston Clinton	11/13	Flamstead	20
Aston Hill (Bucks)	11	Frogmore (Herts)	30
Barton-le-Clay	26	Gaddesden Row	18
Bedmond	2	Galley Hill	29
Bellingdon	6	Great Gaddesden	18
Bendish	30	Great Hampden	9
Berkhamsted	16/17	Great Kimble	10
Berkhamsted Common	17	Great Missenden	8
Bidwell	24	Great Offley	28
Blow's Down	21		
Botley (Bucks)	4	Hale, The	12
Bourne End (Herts)	16	Halton	11
Bovingdon (Herts)	16	Hampden Bottom	9
Breachwood Green	30	Hampden Row	9
Buckland (Bucks)	13	Harlington (Beds)	25
Buckland Common	5	Hastoe	5
Butterfield Green	29	Hawridge	5
		Hemel Hempstead	3/19
Caddington	21	High Down	27
Cassiobury Park	1	Hitchin	27/28
Chalgrave	24	Houghton Regis	24
Charlton (Herts)	28	Hyde End	7
Chartridge	6	Hyde Heath	7
Chesham	4/6/7		
Chipperfield	3	Ickleford	27
Chivery	12	Incombe Hole	14
Cholesbury	5	Ivinghoe	14
Crong, The	12	Ivinghoe Aston	14
Croxley Green	1	Ivinghoe Beacon	14

Walks

Jacotts Hill	1
Jockey End	18
King's Langley	2/3
King's Walden	30
Lanes End	12
Ley Hill	4
Lilley Bottom	30
Little Green	1
Little Hampden	9
Lovett's End	19
Lower Cadsden	10
Luton	29
Maiden Bower	23
Markyate	20
Minsbury Hill	28
Mobwell	8
Monks Risborough	10
New Ground	15
Offley Bottom	28
Offley Cross	28
Paines End	12
Pascomb Pit	22
Pepperstock	20
Pepsal End	20
Piccott's End	19
Pirton	27
Pitstone Hill	14
Potten End	17
Prestwood	8/9
Pulpit Hill	10
Punch's Cross	27
Puttenham	13

Walks

Ravensburgh Castle	26
St. Leonards	12
Sewell	23
Sharpenhoe Clappers	25
Steps Hill	14
Stopsley	29
Stopsley Common	29
Sundon Hills	25
The Crong	12
The Hale	12
Thorn	24
Tom's Hill	15
Totternhoe	23
Totternhoe Knolls	23
Tring Station	15
Two Waters	3
Tyler's Hill	4
Upper Sundon	25
Warden Hill	29
Water End (Herts)	19
Watford	1
Wendover	11
Wendover Woods	11/12
Whipsnade Down	22
White End	4
Whiteleaf	10
Whiteway Bottom	30
Wilstone	13
Wilstone Reservoir	13
Wingfield	24

Books Published by
THE BOOK CASTLE

COUNTRYSIDE CYCLING IN BEDFORDSHIRE,
BUCKINGHAMSHIRE AND HERTFORDSHIRE:
Mick Payne.
Twenty rides on- and off-road for all the family.

PUB WALKS FROM COUNTRY STATIONS:
Bedfordshire and Hertfordshire: Clive Higgs.
Fourteen circular country rambles, each starting and finishing at a
railway station and incorporating a pub-stop at a mid-way point.

LOCAL WALKS: South Bedfordshire and North Chilterns:
Vaughan Basham.
Twenty-seven thematic circular walks.

LOCAL WALKS: North and Mid Bedfordshire:
Vaughan Basham.
Twenty-five thematic circular walks.

FAMILY WALKS: Chilterns South: Nick Moon.
Twenty rides on- and off-road for all the family.

CHILTERN WALKS: Hertfordshire, Bedfordshire and
North Buckinghamshire: Nick Moon.
CHILTERN WALKS: Buckinghamshire: Nick Moon.
CHILTERN WALKS: Oxfordshire and West Buckinghamshire:
Nick Moon.
A trilogy of circular walks, in association with the Chiltern Society.
Each volume contains 30 circular walks.

OXFORDSHIRE WALKS:
Oxford, the Cotswolds and the Cherwell Valley: Nick Moon.
OXFORDSHIRE WALKS:
Oxford, the Downs and the Thames Valley: Nick Moon.
Two volumes that complement Chiltern Walks: Oxfordshire and
complete coverage of the county, in association with the Oxford
Fieldpaths Society. Thirty circular walks in each.

JOURNEYS INTO BEDFORDSHIRE: Anthony Mackay.
Foreword by The Marquess of Tavistock, Woburn Abbey. A lavish
book of over 150 evocative ink drawings.

MANORS and MAYHEM, PAUPERS and PARSONS: Tales from Four Shire: Beds., Bucks., Herts., and Northants.: John Houghton
Little-known historical snippets and stories.

MYTHS and WITCHES, PEOPLE and POLITICS: Tales from Four Shires: Bucks., Beds., Herts., and Northants.: John Houghton.
Anthology of strange, but true historical events.

HISTORIC FIGURES IN THE BUCKINGHAMSHIRE LANDSCAPE: John Houghton.
Major personalities and events that have shaped the county's past, including a special section on Bletchley Park.

FOLK: Characters and Events in the History of Bedfordshire and Northamptonshire: Vivienne Evans.
Anthology about people of yesteryear – arranged alphabetically by village or town.

BEDFORDSHIRE'S YESTERYEARS Vol 2:
The Rural Scene: Brenda Fraser Newstead.
Vivid first-hand accounts of country life two or three generations ago.

BEDFORDSHIRE'S YESTERYEARS Vol 3:
Craftsmen and Tradespeople: Brenda Fraser Newstead.
Fascinating recollections over several generations practising many vanishing crafts and trades.

BEDFORDSHIRE'S YESTERYEARS Vol 4:
Wat Times and Civil Matters: Brenda Fraser Newstead.
Two World Wars, plus transport, law and order, etc.

THE RAILWAY AGE IN BEDFORDSHIRE: Fred Cockman.
Classic, illustrated account of early railway history.

GLEANINGS REVISITED:
Nostalgic Thoughts of a Bedfordshire Farmer's Boy:
E W O'Dell.
His own sketches and early photographs adorn this lively account of rural Bedfordshire in days gone by.

FARM OF MY CHILDHOOD, 1925–1947: Mary Roberts.
An almost vanished lifestyle on a remote farm near Flitwick.

SWANS IN MY KITCHEN: Lis Dorer.
Story of a Swan Sanctuary near Hemel Hempstead.

DUNSTABLE WITH THE PRIORY: 1100–1550: Vivienne Evans.
Dramatic growth of Henry I's important new town around a major crossroads.

DUNSTABLE DECADE: THE EIGHTIES:
A Collection of Photographs: Pat Lovering.
A souvenir book of nearly 300 pictures of people and events in the 1980s.

DUNSTABLE IN DETAIL: Nigel Benson.
A hundred of the town's buildings and features, plus town trail map.

OLD DUNSTABLE: Bill Twaddle.
A new edition of this collection of early photographs.

BOURNE and BRED: A Dunstable Boyhood Between the Wars:
Colin Bourne.
An elegantly written, well-illustrated book capturing the spirit of the town over fifty years ago.

ROYAL HOUGHTON: Pat Lovering:
Illustrated history of Houghton Regis from the earliest times to the present.

THE CHANGING FACE OF LUTON: An Illustrated History:
Stephen Bunker, Robin Holgate and Marian Nichols.
Luton's development from earliest times to the present busy industrial town. Illustrated in colour and monochrome

THE MEN WHO WORE STRAW HELMETS:
Policing Luton, 1840–1974: Tom Madigan.
Meticulously chronicled history; dozens of rare photographs; author served in Luton Police for fifty years.

BETWEEN THE HILLS: The Story of Lilley, a Chiltern Village:
Roy Pinnock.
A priceless piece of our heritage – the rural beauty remains but the customs and way of life described here have largely disappeared.

A HATTER GOES MAD!: Kristina Howells.
Luton Town footballers, officials and supporters talk to a female fan.

LEGACIES: Tales and Legends of Luton and the North Chilterns:
Vic Lea.
Twenty-five mysteries and stories based on fact, including Luton Town Football Club. Many photographs.

LEAFING THROUGH LITERATURE:
Writers' Lives in Hertfordshire and Bedfordshire:
David Carroll.
Illustrated short biographies of many famous authors and their connections with these counties.

A PILGRIMAGE IN HERTFORDSHIRE: H M Alderman.
Classic, between-the-wars tour round the county, embellished with line drawings.

CHILTERN ARCHAEOLOGY: RECENT WORK:
A Handbook for the Next Decade: edited by Robin Holgate.
The latest views, results and excavations by twenty-three leading archaeologists throughout the Chilterns.

THE HILL OF THE MARTYR:
An Architectural History of St. Albans Abbey: Eileen Roberts.
Scholarly and readable chronological narrative history of Hertfordshire and Bedfordshire's famous cathedral. Fully illustrated with photographs and plans.

THE TALL HITCHIN SERGEANT:
A Victorian Crime Novel Based on Fact: Edgar Newman.
Mixes real police officers and authentic background with an exciting storyline.

THE TALL HITCHIN INSPECTOR'S CASEBOOK:
A Victorian Crime Novel Based on Fact: Edgar Newman.
Worthies of the time encounter more archetypal villains.

SPECIALLY FOR CHILDREN

VILLA BELOW THE KNOLLS: A Story of Roman Britain:
Michael Dundrow.
An exciting adventure for young John in Totternhoe and Dunstable two thousand years ago.

THE RAVENS: One Boy Against the Might of Rome:
James Dyer.
On the Barton Hills and in the south-east of England as the men of the great fort of Ravensburgh (near Hexton) confront the invaders.

Further titles are in preparation.
All the above are available via any bookshop, or from the publisher and bookseller

THE BOOK CASTLE
12 Church Street, Dunstable Bedfordshire, LU5 4RU
Tel: (01582) 605670